Reflections

Around the table of the King

Meditations on the communion service from a Jewish perspective

With a
Foreword by
Martin
Goldsmith

John Jacobs *with Gill Jacobs*

Endorsement

In an upper room in Jerusalem (the location is now lost), the Lord Jesus instigated a special memorial meal to be celebrated by his people until he comes again at the conclusion of history, when his people will meet with him at the Marriage Supper of the Lamb. In this excellent book, John Jacobs, using his Jewish heritage and knowledge, takes us through the events and their meaning from the Passover and supernatural escape from Egyptian captivity to enrich our understanding of the Lord's Table.

I highly recommend this book as it shows the solid historical foundation of the Christian faith and what these things mean for us today. I pray that it will have a wide readership, and that many will come to a fuller understanding of the love Jesus has for them.

Clive Anderson, pastor, author and tour guide leader

John Jacobs, a Jewish disciple of Jesus, has performed a great service to both the church and the Jewish people by bringing together a wonderful treasury of prayers, hymns, songs and his own reflections to enhance our appreciation and celebration of that most Jewish of meals, the Christian service of communion. Just as Yeshua (Jesus) instructed his disciples to 'do this in remembrance of me', so Jacobs, with this rich collection of resources, helps us to remember, reflect on and rejoice in what God has done for us in sending his Son, the Messiah of Israel and Saviour of all nations.

Dr Richard Harvey, Senior Researcher, Jews for Jesus UK

© Day One Publications 2021
First Edition 2021

Unless otherwise indicated, Scripture quotations in this publication are taken from the Holy
Bible, New International Version (NIV), copyright © 1973, 1978, 1984, 2011 by International
Bible Society. Used by permission of Hodder & Stoughton Publishers, A member of the
Hodder Headline Group. All rights reserved. "NIV" is a registered trademark of International
Bible Society. UK trademark number 1448790.

British Library Cataloguing in Publication Data available

ISBN 978-1-84625-681-3

Published by Day One Publications
Ryelands Road, Leominster, HR6 8NZ

☎ 01568 613 740
FAX: 01568 611 473
email—sales@dayone.co.uk
web site—www.dayone.co.uk

Cover designed by Kathryn Chedgzoy and printed by 4Edge

For Phil and Peggy,
who first pointed me to Jesus the Messiah

So we share in this Bread of life,
And we drink of His sacrifice,
As a sign of our bonds of peace,
Around the table of the King.
(Stuart Townend, Keith & Kristyn Getty,
'Behold the Lamb Who Bears Our Sins
Away', © 2007 Thankyou Music)

Contents

Foreword

Making attractive use of his Jewish family and synagogue background, John and Gill Jacobs share with us the Jewish roots of Christian faith and worship, particularly of the Lord's Supper, the Table of the King.

This book develops the theme that the origins of the Holy Communion, the Lord's Supper, lie in the Jewish Passover. This reality can be easily overlooked in our churches. Christians sometimes attend only to the historical development of Holy Communion after New Testament times and the different understandings of the sacrament in Roman Catholic, Lutheran, Anglican and Reformed traditions. This can have unfortunate consequences. The warmth of a memorial meal together is replaced by just a formal liturgy.

Leaving its Passover roots behind, the Anglican Church has laid down that only an ordained person can lead communion. With the increasing shortage of ordained people in many countries, this puts an unacceptable workload on our ministers and prevents them from having adequate time and energy for their calling to pastor, teach and train their congregations. And at times such as in the current pandemic, it may prevent Christians from the joy and grace of this act of remembering the sacrificial death of Jesus for us. So in my view, I believe we should follow the Passover model of partaking of bread and wine in our homes with a few friends or just as families. And of course it would be good to do so in the context of a meal; as American Thanksgiving, Chinese New Year and Christmas show, a special meal has significance. Throughout Scripture, eating together is seen to be important in relationships. For Jewish Christians or messianic believers, a traditional communion service can come as a bit of a shock. Holy Communion/the Lord's Supper is often referred to as 'this feast', but participants receive only a tiny piece of leavened bread (leaven is a biblical symbol of sin and should be removed from the house over Passover) and the tiniest taste of wine (sometimes even diluted with water!).

Around the Table of the King will not only introduce its readers to the riches of Jewish life and culture, but will also warm our hearts with its spiritual emphasis. Each of the thirty-four short chapters closes with something devotional: a prayer, a biblical thought or a quotation.

I warmly recommend this book to all, with its balanced and warm-hearted Jewish content and its clear biblical and spiritual character. A big 'thank you' to John and Gill!

Martin Goldsmith,

Lecturer, All Nations Christian College, Ware

Preface

As a Jew who came to faith in Jesus as a young man, sharing the communion service with other believers has always been a very precious time for me. It has a resonance that is perhaps sometimes missed by my Christian brothers and sisters who were not brought up in a Jewish home.

All the Old Testament festivals were instituted by God as a way of reminding Israelites in every generation of their deliverance by God from Egypt and His continuing care. But, more importantly, the feasts are significant in that they foreshadowed the coming Messiah. Much of Jesus' public ministry took place in conjunction with the festivals ordained by God.

Often the link between Passover and communion is missed, and as a result I believe our experience of gathering around the table of the Lord is weaker.

My hope in putting together these meditations is that I can share some of the thoughts I have had over the years as I have been privileged to lead communion services as well as Passover celebrations at various places and times in my life.

If others find these meditations useful as they lead communion, I shall be glad.

John Jacobs

Around the table of the King

Invitation

This is the table not of the Church but of the Lord.
It is to be made ready for those who love him,
and who want to love him more.
So, come, you who have much faith
and you who have little,
You who have been here often and you who
have not been for a very long time,
You who have tried to follow and you who have failed.
Come, not because it is I who invite you:
It is our Lord. It is his will that those who want him
should meet him here.
(From the Iona Community)[1]

Perfect
sacrifice

From the beginning of time the Bible records how sacrifice was ordained by God and instituted by Him. It began with Adam and ended with Jesus, the second Adam.

Adam and Eve had been warned that death would be the result of their disobedience. But they had never seen death and so didn't know what it was like until they saw an animal killed to 'cover' their sin of disobedience: 'The LORD God made garments of skin . . . and clothed them' (Gen. 3:21).

The need for this only makes sense as we consider the nature of God: awful and terrible in His purity and dreadful in His anger against all unrighteousness. Sin has to be atoned for if God is to be God. The writer of Hebrews puts it very plainly: 'without the shedding of blood there is no forgiveness' (Heb. 9:22).

So, throughout the Old Testament, we follow this theme. At Mount Sinai God gave Moses instructions in the various offerings that would be necessary for Israel to come near to God. Sacrifices had to be made continually for the sins of the people: animals with no defects constantly dying in order to cover the guilt of the children of Israel.

The theme of the need for a sacrifice to cover sin continues throughout Scripture. The account of Abraham and Isaac gives us a faint clue as to the enormity of what God did to provide salvation for us.

God had given Abraham and Sarah a son in their old age and promised that through his descendants all nations would be blessed. Now Abraham was being told to prepare to sacrifice this precious son. But God was not asking him to do something He would not do Himself! Just as Isaac was bound, so Jesus was bound and laid on the cross of wood. But there was no ram to stand in for Him. He was the Lamb of God, in our place!

So it was that sacrifices continued until the perfect sacrifice was made. It was not long after Jesus gave His life as a sacrifice that the temple was destroyed so that, in God's sovereignty, animal sacrifices could no longer be performed.

Jesus Christ came to become the final and complete sacrifice for our sins. When He died on the cross, all our sins were laid on Him, and He died in our place. No further sacrifice is needed—because Christ gave His life for us. When we put our faith and trust in Him, the Bible says that 'we have been made holy through the sacrifice of the body of Jesus Christ once for all' (Heb. 10:10).

If we were sinless, no sacrifice would have been necessary; but praise God that Christ's sacrifice paid for all my sins and yours, past, present and future. Sin had to be punished, atonement for our sins required the shedding of blood, and our Saviour took the punishment that should have been ours. We are ransomed through His blood shed for us on the cross. That is why we are here: to remember.

As we come to these reminders of Jesus' body and blood, it is good for us to recognize and acknowledge that it was because of our sins that the sacrifice was necessary. We proclaim our faith in and gratitude to God for that perfect sacrifice that was made once for all. And we rejoice that, because of Jesus, we can draw near to God in loving relationship.

Prayer

> *Merciful God, we confess that we have not loved you with our whole heart.*
> *We have failed to be an obedient people.*
> *We have not done your will.*
> *We have broken your laws. We have rebelled against your love.*
> *We have not loved our neighbours, and we have not heard the cry of the needy.*
> *Forgive us we pray.*
> *Free us from our sins so that we may live in joyful obedience,*
> *Through Jesus Christ our Lord,*
> *Amen.*
> *(United Methodist Book of Worship)*[1]

Preparation

On the first Sunday in August, the month before the Jewish New Year, Jews make preparations for the High Holy Days: New Year (Rosh Hashanah) and the Day of Atonement (Yom Kippur).

The concept of repentance and of the need to repent is very strong in the Jewish tradition. Jews believe that since the sacrificial system no longer exists, 'by prayer, repentance and charity' God's favour (forgiveness) can be obtained. So it is strange that with such an emphasis on repentance, it is really only during the New Year season that most Jews think about penitence. Why is this?

It is because, as the Hebrew calendar draws to a close, Jews are called to remember that this is the time when God draws up the accounts at the end of the old year.

> Jews believe that God balances a person's good deeds [*mitzvot*] over the last year against their bad deeds, and decides what the next year will be like for them. God records the judgement in the Book of Life, where he sets out who is going to live, who is going to die, who will have a good time and who will have a bad time during the next year. The book and the judgement are finally sealed on Yom Kippur.[1]

The early Jewish Christians had to learn a different understanding of forgiveness. Their emphasis on obedience to the law was replaced by the understanding that they would never be able to earn forgiveness by the quantity or quality of their 'prayer, penitence or charity'. Nothing they could do would ever be good enough.

As Paul expressed it in Romans 7:7 and 9: 'I would not have known what sin was had it not been for the law. For I would not have known what coveting really was if the law had not said, "You shall not covet" . . . Once I was alive apart from the law; but when the commandment came, sin sprang to life and I died.'

We know that the price of our forgiveness has been paid on the cross. Because Jesus bore in Himself the judgement we deserve, our relationship with God is different from the Jew's. For us as Christians we see God as father-like rather than magisterial.

It is traditional, every time we come to the table of the Lord, to prepare for communion by confession and repentance. We are called to keep short accounts with God.

Yet, although it is important to reflect regularly on our lives and to repent of our failings, the Lord's Supper is not a meal of repentance. It is a feast of joy where we celebrate the liberating and life-giving forgiveness of God. Let no one who is trusting in Christ for salvation and is seeking to walk in His ways exclude him- or herself from this table.

> The price is paid,
> Come let us enter in
> To all that Jesus died
> To make our own.
> For every sin

More than enough He gave
And bought our freedom
From each guilty stain.

The price is paid
Alleluia
Amazing grace
So strong and sure
And so with all my heart
My life in every part
I live to thank You for
The price You paid.
(Graham Kendrick, 1983)

The table of our Lord is here. Before us is a simple meal of bread and wine which reminds us of the broken body and shed blood of the Lord Jesus Christ: the price that was paid once and for all for our forgiveness.

Prayer

Father of all,
we give you thanks and praise,
that when we were still far off
you met us in your Son and brought us home.
Dying and living, he declared your love,
gave us grace, and opened the gate of glory.
May we who share Christ's body live his risen life;
we who drink his cup bring life to others;
we whom the Spirit lights give light to the world.

Keep us firm in the hope you have set before us,
so we and all your children shall be free,
and the whole earth live to praise your name;
through Christ our Lord, Amen.
('Prayer after Communion')[2]

Rosh Hashanah:
Sound the trumpet

We celebrate the Jewish New Year around September. It is called Rosh Hashanah, and Jews believe that on this day individuals and the entire world are held in judgement. 'New Year isn't only celebrated in the synagogue, but at home too. A special [family] meal is served, with the emphasis on sweetness' to usher in the New Year. It is the custom, before the evening meal, to dip an apple in honey, symbolizing the Jews' hopes for a sweet and fruitful year.[1]

Also, 'there's often a pomegranate on the table because of a tradition that pomegranates have 613 seeds, one for each of the commandments that a Jew is obliged to keep'.[2] The standard greeting at the meal is, 'May you be inscribed in the Book of Life for a happy year.'

Rosh Hashanah is celebrated over two days and marks the first two days of the '10 days of awe' leading up to the holiest day in the Jewish calendar, the Day of Atonement. This is a time when Jews consider the judgement of God on them for the past year.

In the Old Testament the New Year is also called *Yom Teruah*, which means 'Day of Trumpets'; the central feature of this festival in the synagogue is the sounding of the *shophar*, a ram's horn which is blown 100 times in a particular rhythm (Lev. 23:24). The sound was heard on many important occasions in Bible times, warning people that a battle was approaching or reassuring them that hostilities had stopped.

The ram's horn is blown today for two reasons: one is to call the people to repentance, and the other is to warn that

God's day of reckoning is at hand. The sound of the ram's horn recalls the binding of Isaac, when a ram was offered up in his stead—an event that, according to tradition, occurred on Rosh Hashanah.

Today on Rosh Hashanah Jews are still called to repentance and will consider God's judgement on sin. They will state their sincere intention to follow God's path and lead a good life so that their names will be recorded in the Book of Life. They will give to charity and spend the next ten days in penitence and prayer as they seek to atone for the sins of the past year.

It is tragic that so many Jews are blind to the truth about Jesus. For us, the parallel between the ram dying in Isaac's place and Jesus dying in ours is so clear. We also know about the day of judgement that will surely come when God wraps up history. We too have been called to repentance and to live a good life. And like sincere Jews, we long for our names to be written in the Book of Life.

But we gather around this communion table as believers in Jesus the Messiah and we have an assurance that Jews without Jesus do not have. We are resting in the eternal life that we received when we put our faith in Him. Without His death and resurrection and without the Holy Spirit who was given at Pentecost, we would be left with nothing more than a sincere hope.

Jesus tells us that when He returns in power and glory there will be a loud trumpet call (Matt. 24:31) and judgement will follow. When that time comes we will be secure in the knowledge that our sins have been dealt with and that our names are written in the Lamb's Book of Life.

Blessed assurance, Jesus is mine!

Oh what a foretaste of glory divine!

. . .

Watching and waiting, looking above,

Filled with His goodness, lost in His love.

This is my story, this is my song,

Praising my Saviour, all the day long;

This is my story, this is my song,

Praising my Saviour, all the day long.

(Fanny Crosby, 1873)

So as we come to this remembrance feast, may it truly be a 'day of awe' as we consider Jesus—our High Priest who fulfilled the temple sacrifices and made eternal atonement for us—and as we come to Him in full assurance of faith.

Prayer

Father in heaven, we praise You that we can come to You in confidence knowing that our names are written in the Lamb's Book of Life. Thank You for the assurance we have, not just for this year, but for eternity. We come praising Jesus for the direct access to Your throne He provides. We rejoice in Christ's promise that He will never forget or forsake those who have come to Him. Thank You that there is no uncertainty! Amen.

Of first
importance

Much of our day-to-day life is taken up with working to earn money and considering how best to save and invest for the future. Of course, this is necessary, but in our materialistic society it is easy for this to take over the focus of our lives.

During the season of Rosh Hashanah and Yom Kippur, the blowing of the *shophar*, the ram's horn, calls Jews to number their days. As they ask for their names to be written in the Book of Life, they think about time and how they use it, and about life and how they use that. The *shophar* is seen as God's alarm clock, waking us up from the 'slumber' in which we spend our days to consider what is of first importance.

Down through the centuries God calls to His creation through his Word, urging us to put our security and hope in the things that will last. More than six hundred years before Jesus, the prophet Isaiah asked a question that is still relevant today:

> Why spend money on what is not bread,
>> and your labour on what does not satisfy?
> Listen, listen to me, and eat what is good,
>> and you will delight in the richest of fare.
> Give ear and come to me;
>> listen, that you may live. (Isa. 55:2–3)

In Old Testament times, just as in our time, people were busy trying to make their lives on earth more comfortable. They, like us, saw their security in savings in the bank, in their homes and in their possessions. But Isaiah is saying: Listen!

Think about what is of greatest importance. Money and possessions will not satisfy the hunger of the soul.

Jesus explained it more clearly by the shores of Galilee. As recorded in John 6, the crowd of people had just seen the miracle of the feeding of the five thousand, but they still wanted Jesus to show them a sign: 'What sign then will you give that we may see it and believe you?' (John 6:30). The people reminded Jesus of the manna that was given to their forefathers in the wilderness. They wanted something material, and didn't want to hear about the true bread from heaven given by God to give life to the world.

> I am the bread of life. Whoever comes to me will never go hungry, and whoever believes in me will never be thirsty. But as I told you, you have seen me and still you do not believe . . . Whoever eats this bread will live for ever. This bread is my flesh, which I will give for the life of the world . . . Your ancestors ate manna and died, but whoever feeds on this bread will live for ever. (John 6:35, 51, 58)

Paul tells us what is of first importance in 1 Corinthians 15:3–4: 'that Christ died for our sins according to the Scriptures, that he was buried, that he was raised on the third day according to the Scriptures'.

> This sacred feast is medicine to the sick, comfort to the sinner and bounty to the poor; while to the healthy, the righteous, and the rich, if any such could be found,

it would be of no value. For while Christ is therein given us for food, we see that without him we fail and waste away, just as hunger destroys the vigour of the body. Next, as he is given for life, we understand that without him we are certainly dead.[1]

So, as we come to the table of the Lord, let us remind ourselves of the futility of trusting in our own resources both for this life and for the life to come. Our boast must be in the death of Christ our God.

Prayer

> *Jesus, be the centre*
> *Be my source, be my light . . .*
> *Be my hope, be my song . . .*
> *Be the fire in my heart*
> *Be the wind in these sails . . .*
> *Be the reason that I live . . .*
> *Be my path, be my guide*
> *Jesus*
> (Michael Frye © 1999 Vineyard Songs)

Lord, be our only confidence and hope, our riches and our joy, now and for ever. Amen.

Days of
Remembrance

Seek the LORD while he may be found;
    call on him while he is near.
Let the wicked forsake their ways
    and the unrighteous their thoughts.
Let them turn to the LORD, and he will have mercy on
    them,
    and to our God, for he will freely pardon. (Isa. 55:6–7)

The season in the Jewish calendar between Rosh Hashanah and Yom Kippur is called 'Days of Remembrance'. These ten days that begin at Rosh Hashanah are also known as days of repentance, or days of awe, ushering in the final phase of atonement. This is a time to remember the final judgement when we must give account to God the Almighty Judge. Jewish people spend these days considering the year that has passed, thinking about their conduct, and coming in prayer and penitence before God, seeking His forgiveness for any sin they may have committed against God or man.

This practice is a good one. We all need to spend time meditating on our lives, considering whether we are walking in God's will and where we need to seek His Spirit to bring about change. We need to remind ourselves that without His work on the cross we would still be enslaved to sin and under God's judgement. And we need times when we recommit ourselves to our Lord Jesus.

In the Bible, 'remembering' is not the recalling of something forgotten, but the enacting of something promised; a covenant that formally binds two parties in a relationship.

Modern-day Jews still look to the Mosaic covenant—what we call the old covenant—for their guidance. They are required to obey God and keep the law, and in return they believe He will protect them and bless them (Deut. 30:15–18).

One of the earliest-recorded covenants between God and man was given after the flood. God made a covenant with the earth that He would never again bring a worldwide flood, and He gave the rainbow as a sign of that promise.

Just as the rainbow in the sky brings to our mind God's promise not to flood the earth, so, as we gather round the communion table, the cup brings to our mind the new covenant.

In the new covenant, things change. Instead of us having to take action to obey the law, now God is the one who takes action to secure our salvation and blessing, and He writes His law on our hearts.

> Nothing in my hand I bring,
> Simply to Thy cross I cling;
> Naked, come to Thee for dress;
> Helpless, look to Thee for grace:
> Foul, I to the fountain fly;
> Wash me, Saviour, or I die.
> (Augustus Toplady, 1740–1872, 'Rock of Ages')

'After the supper [Jesus] took the cup, saying, "This cup is the new covenant in my blood, which is poured out for you"' (Luke 22:20). As we eat and drink we recall God's promise that all who trust in Jesus will receive forgiveness and eternal life—

life that includes life before death as well as life after death. The life we have now and the life we look forward to are both part of the covenant promise of God.

For us at the communion service today this also is a day of remembrance. But there is no sacrifice here. Each time we meet with Christians at this table we remember what Christ has done for us, and by faith we meet Him also. We come to celebrate the fact that there is a new covenant in His blood and that all those covenant promises are ours. There is no condemnation for those who are in Christ Jesus! God is our God, and we are His people.

The bread and wine are before us to remind us of both the sacrifice and the promise.

Prayer

Lord and Father, thank You that when we were far from You, You met us, prodigals as we were, and brought us to Yourself. Thank You for the Lord Jesus Christ who in life and in death showed us Your love and opened the way to salvation. Thank You that on that last day we will be able to stand before You clothed in His righteousness.

Keep us firm and steadfast in that faith You have planted in us so that our lives may bring others to You, and bring praise and glory to your name. Amen.

Atonement: Yom Kippur

The life of a creature is in the blood, and I have given it
to you to make atonement for yourselves on the altar;
it is the blood that makes atonement for one's life.
(Lev. 17:11)

The tenth day after the festival of Rosh Hashanah is a most solemn day in the Jewish year when God's judgements drawn up during the previous ten days are believed to be sealed in the Book of Life. It is called Yom Kippur, or the Day of Atonement, and it usually falls around October.

On this day, Jews everywhere fast and pray to be cleansed of the sins of the past year. They believe that fasting itself cannot secure forgiveness but must be accompanied by sincere repentance and a firm resolve to make amends for the past and to lead a noble life.

In Bible times, as now, this was the most holy day for the children of Israel. Special sacrifices for sin were made and the high priest went alone into the Holy of Holies to make atonement for the people of Israel. After AD 70, when the temple was destroyed, there was no longer a high priest and no animal sacrifices could be made. Since that time, blood sacrifices have been replaced with penitence, prayer and charity.

In temple times the high priest made three sacrifices of atonement: for himself and his family; for the priests; and for the household of Israel. The Day of Atonement was a reminder that daily, weekly and monthly sacrifices in the temple were not sufficient. Perfect atonement had not been provided. When the high priest went into the Holy of Holies he had no certainty of acceptance, and was aware that he was risking his life when entering. 'The LORD said to Moses: "Tell your brother Aaron that he is not to come whenever he chooses into the Most Holy Place behind the curtain in front of the atonement cover on the ark, or else he will die. For I will appear in the cloud over the atonement cover"' (Lev. 16:2).

There is a legend among Orthodox Jews based on the writings in the *Zohar*, one of the Jewish commentaries on the Torah, that before the high priest entered the Holy of Holies to sprinkle the blood sacrifice on the ark, a rope would be tied around his ankle. It was said that if his sins were not atoned for properly, or he was not properly prepared according to divine instructions, he would die in the presence of the *shekinah* glory of God. Since nobody else could enter that part of the temple without also dying, the priests felt they needed a way to retrieve the body of the high priest if necessary. That was the purpose of the rope: to drag his body out. Although there is doubt over the reliability of this legend, it is clear that there was a great deal of concern about the possibility of a priest being found unworthy and the fear of needing to enter the most holy area.

Even today, when Jews celebrate the Day of Atonement, there is the same uncertainty of acceptance. They have no assurance that their prayers for their names to be written in the Book of Life for the coming year will be answered.

Jewish people who have not received their Messiah are still living in the fear of the wrath of God. When they pray for forgiveness, there is no guarantee they will be pardoned.

How different for us who belong to Christ!

> [Jesus] did not enter by means of the blood of
> goats and calves; but he entered the Most Holy
> Place once for all by his own blood, so obtaining
> eternal redemption. The blood of goats and bulls
> and the ashes of a heifer sprinkled on those who are
> ceremonially unclean sanctify them so that they are
> outwardly clean. How much more, then, will the
> blood of Christ, who through the eternal Spirit offered
> himself unblemished to God, cleanse our consciences
> from acts that lead to death, so that we may serve
> the living God! For this reason Christ is the mediator
> of a new covenant, that those who are called may
> receive the promised eternal inheritance—now that
> he has died as a ransom to set them free from the sins
> committed under the first covenant. (Heb. 9:12–15)

We come in obedience to Christ who died in our place as the perfect sacrifice, acceptable to God, making atonement for our sins once for all time. We come knowing that, 'if we confess our sins, he is faithful and just and will forgive us our sins and purify us from all unrighteousness' (1 John 1:9).

> Guilty, vile, and helpless we;
> Spotless Lamb of God was He;
> 'Full atonement!'—can it be?
> Hallelujah! What a Saviour!
> (Philip Bliss, 'Man of Sorrows', 1875)

Prayer

> *Almighty God, our heavenly Father:*
> *in your tender mercy*
> *you gave your only Son Jesus Christ*
> *to suffer death upon the cross for our redemption;*
> *he made there*
> *a full atonement for the sins of the whole world,*
> *offering once for all his one sacrifice of himself;*
> *he instituted,*
> *and in his holy gospel commanded us to continue,*
> *a perpetual memory of his precious death*
> *until he comes again.*
> (Book of Common Prayer)

Thank You, our God, that You forgive all our sins, pardon all our iniquities, and grant atonement for all our transgressions through Jesus. Amen.

Atonement: Yom Kippur

Meals
matter

Recently I noticed something in Exodus that I had never seen before. The passage is a familiar one, where Moses tells the people of Israel the commands he had received from God on Mount Sinai.

> Then [Moses] took the Book of the Covenant and read it to the people. They responded, 'We will do everything the Lord has said; we will obey.' Moses then took the blood, sprinkled it on the people and said, 'This is the blood of the covenant that the Lord has made with you in accordance with all these words.' Moses and Aaron, Nadab and Abihu, and the seventy elders of Israel went up and saw the God of Israel. Under his feet was something like a pavement made of lapis lazuli, as bright blue as the sky. But God did not raise his hand against these leaders of the Israelites; they saw God, and they ate and drank. (Exod. 24:7–11)

This passage tells of God's covenant with his people who confirm their intention to obey. Then the blood of sacrifice is sprinkled on them. The portion I had not noticed before was the account of Moses, the priests and the seventy elders all ascending Mount Sinai and eating a meal in the presence of God! What was significant in this event was that they were not consumed. God did not 'break out' against them.

Meals matter. They are not just symbolic, but are also a sign of fellowship. We know we can't eat with someone with whom we are at enmity.

The early Christians met together regularly, often in each

other's houses and at other times in a place of worship, to 'break bread' (share a meal) and remember Christ's covenant promise to be with them always, to the end of the age. It was a joyful, informal meal that bonded the church, minimizing social differences, keeping alive the memory of Jesus' life, but looking forward in anticipation to the coming of Christ's kingdom.

Sadly, in our individualistic society here in the West, we have lost some of that experience of community those early believers felt. But we too share a common sense of wonder at the power of God in the resurrection of Christ and the grace of God in forgiving our sins and calling us together as a church. And we are still called to care for and support one another as members of the body of Christ.

> As we are gathered, Jesus is here;
> One with each other, Jesus is here;
> Joined by the Spirit, washed in the blood,
> Part of the body, the Church of God . . .
> (John Daniels © 1979 Authentic Publishing)

There appears to be a connecting theme in Bible history of covenant promises, the shedding of blood, and a meal with God. There are parallels between the events on Mount Sinai and those at the Last Supper on the night before Jesus died. At that meal, Jesus instituted a new covenant which again was confirmed through the shedding of blood—this time, His own.

As we celebrate this communion meal, we look back, and also forward. We look back to the old covenant before the coming of Jesus, and see how the seriousness of sin meant constant sacrifices of animals and the shedding of their blood to make atonement. We also look back at Christ's sacrifice for our sin, His blood shed once for all, reconciling us to God and confirming His new covenant with us.

But we also look forward to the time when the covenant will be fulfilled in the kingdom of God (Luke 22:16). This fulfilment is what we eagerly wait for: what is called the 'marriage supper of the Lamb'. We, the bride of Christ, will eat and drink in God's presence, not at a distance but sitting with Him. No need for any further sacrifice: the price has been paid, the new covenant fulfilled!

Prayer

Heavenly Father, thank You for this meal of remembrance. Thank You that You are the covenant-keeping God who delights to show steadfast love and to forgive us as we come to You.

As Your covenant people, may our souls always hunger after You. May our hearts seek You and find You; and may our lives of service bring praise and glory to Your name. Amen.

Passover

> We were slaves of Pharaoh in Egypt . . . So the LORD
> brought us out of Egypt with a mighty hand and an
> outstretched arm. (Deut. 6:21; 26:8)

As we look forward to Easter, Jewish people are looking forward to Passover. This was, and still is, a major festival for the Jews as they look back and recall how God rescued them from slavery in Egypt. It is the most important family festival in the Jewish calendar. Family members dispersed around the country tend to gather together at the family home. The Passover (or Seder) meal for those living outside Israel is celebrated on the first and second day of the festival. (The reason for this is thought to be because in the past, Jewish people outside Israel could not be certain if their local calendars fully conformed to the practice of the temple at Jerusalem, so they added an extra day.)

The Passover feast has been celebrated since Old Testament times. At this meal in Jewish homes now, as then, various things are eaten, drunk and done. Each element of the festival is a visual aid to help us understand the message of the exodus of the Jewish nation from Egypt.

The service takes a set form which is contained in the Haggadah, which is the Hebrew word for 'telling' or 'showing forth'. The Haggadah contains the readings and rituals for the Passover meal going as far back as the second century BC.

The Seder plate contains a lamb bone, representing the sacrificial lamb; bitter herbs, as a reminder of the bitterness of slavery; parsley in salt water, representing freedom; a mixture of apple and nuts shaped to resemble a mud brick; and a hard-boiled egg, a symbol of life and a reminder of the 'voluntary peace offering' from temple times. In addition there is matzah—the unleavened bread—as a reminder of the haste in which the children of Israel left Egypt; and four glasses of wine, representing aspects of the redemption from slavery.

It was no accident that it was at the Passover meal that Jesus gave His followers instructions for the communion service we celebrate today. Passover is the Jewish festival of redemption, when Jewish people remember with thankfulness how they were set free from the physical and political slavery in Egypt.

Nor was it an accident that it was at this meal that Jesus chose to reveal His mission. It was at the Last Supper that Jesus gave new, radical teaching, drawing a parallel between the Jews' redemption from physical slavery in Egypt, and the redemption from slavery to sin that He would bring about through His death on the cross. He wanted His followers to understand that, although physically free from bondage, we are still slaves—in bondage—to our limitations, our faults and our circumstances. And He came to free us from the power of sin and its bonds.

Passover reminded the children of Israel that they could not free themselves. They needed God to act with His mighty hand and outstretched arm. The last plague (the killing of the firstborn), the sacrifice of the lamb and the blood on the doorposts all served to remind them that their salvation came from God.

At communion we too remember that we cannot free ourselves from bondage. We are under God's judgement on sin to which we are enslaved. Nothing we do can make us right with God. In the early church, Peter had to remind members of the church in Jerusalem of this. Some felt the Gentile believers should follow Jewish rules and regulations, but Peter challenged them, asking why they were wanting to impose on others what 'neither we nor our ancestors have been able to bear. No! We believe it is through the grace of our Lord Jesus that we are saved, just as they are' (Acts 15:10–11).

The New Testament refers to Jesus about thirty times as the 'Lamb of God' so that we do not forget that it is only through His death on the cross that we can know forgiveness and the power to overcome sin.

> Because the sinless Saviour died,
> My sinful soul is counted free;
> For God, the Just, is satisfied
> To look on Him and pardon me.
>
> Behold Him there, the risen Lamb,
> My perfect, spotless Righteousness,
> The great unchangeable I AM,
> The King of glory and of grace!
> (Charitie Lees Bancroft, 1841–1892,
> 'Before the Throne of God Above')

For Christians, communion is a festival of redemption as we come to remember the death and resurrection of the Lord

Jesus Christ and to rejoice in our freedom from the slavery and consequences of sin.

Our salvation comes through the sacrifice of Jesus, and, like the children of Israel in Egypt, we are 'covered by the blood of the Lamb'.

Prayer

> *Just as I am, without one plea,*
> *But that Thy blood was shed for me,*
> *And that Thou bid'st me come to Thee,*
> *O Lamb of God, I come!*
>
> *Just as I am, Thou wilt receive,*
> *Wilt welcome, pardon, cleanse, relieve;*
> *Because Thy promise I believe,*
> *O Lamb of God, I come, I come!*
> (Charlotte Elliott, 1835)

Amen.

Our identity
in Christ

Then came the day of Unleavened Bread on which the Passover lamb had to be sacrificed. Jesus sent Peter and John, saying, 'Go and make preparations for us to eat the Passover.' (Luke 22:7)

Jesus was very clear about what should happen on the night we know as the Last Supper on which communion is based. It was to celebrate Passover, the major festival for Jews, looking back and recalling how God had rescued them from slavery in Egypt. The Passover was so important that the Lord Jesus Christ mentions the word 'Passover' five times in Luke 22. Why was it so important? Here are two reasons.

Firstly, the name 'Passover' was a specific reminder of the last plague, the killing of every firstborn in the land—adults, children, animals—except those who had been obedient to God's command and slaughtered a perfect lamb. The last plague in Egypt was the key to the exodus and produced the freeing of the children of Israel from slavery. Their rescue from that plague came about because of the sacrifice of the Passover lamb. The angel of death passed over the homes whose doorposts were marked with the blood of the sacrifice.

As the Israelites applied the blood of the Passover lamb to the doorposts of their homes to save their firstborn sons from death, so we apply the blood of Jesus, the Lamb of God, to the doorposts of our hearts and receive forgiveness and salvation from eternal death. We have been rescued because of the sacrifice of Jesus.

Secondly, the Passover celebration is participatory, not

just observed. Jewish liturgy says that in every generation Jews should see *themselves* as having come out of Egypt. By participating in the celebration, eating, drinking, discussing, the exodus becomes a living reality, shaping the identity of the Jewish people today.

Likewise, when we remember Jesus' cross and resurrection at communion, we participate in the bread and wine and in the meaning and implications of Jesus our paschal lamb. As participation in Passover shapes the identity of the Jews, so participation in the Lord's Supper shapes our identity as Christians.

In John 6 Jesus declared, 'I am the bread of life . . . This bread is my flesh, which I will give for the life of the world' (6:35, 51). He shocked his hearers even more on that occasion by saying, 'Unless you eat the flesh of the Son of Man and drink his blood, you have no life in you. Whoever eats my flesh and drinks my blood has eternal life' (6:53).

We need to understand that here Jesus is not talking literally. 'Eating' in the Scriptures symbolizes appropriation. We partake of His sacrifice ('eat His flesh' and 'drink His blood') by coming to Him and believing on Him. We eat to satisfy our hunger and we drink to satisfy our thirst. Jesus makes this clear: 'Whoever comes to me will never go hungry, and whoever believes in me will never be thirsty' (6:35).

Jesus instituted communion at Passover. When we celebrate communion we celebrate *the* Passover—the perfect sacrifice for us, given once for all. He was telling His disciples in cryptic terms that after His death the paschal lamb would no longer have the same significance. It was the memorial of the historical redemption of the exodus, but only a shadow of the ultimate redemption soon to come—'a better sacrifice' (cf. Heb. 9:23) of death once for all for those who would come to trust in Him: 'But he has appeared once for all at the culmination of the ages to do away with sin by the sacrifice of himself' (Heb. 9:26b).

The new memorial of the bread is of the death, burial and resurrection of Jesus that symbolizes the fulfilment of God's plan for the redemption of all humanity—a greater, eternal redemption.

The Lord gives victory over the devil, feeds us with the bread of life, gives us springs of living water and leads us by the presence of His Holy Spirit.

As we eat the bread we remember, think and meditate on His death and acknowledge that He is all we need to sustain us. As we drink the wine we remember that Christ gave His blood for us, and we partake in His suffering, coming to the cross and dying to ourselves.

Let us celebrate the feast, remembering who we are and whose we are: those redeemed by the blood of Jesus.

Prayer

> *Almighty God,*
> *We thank you for feeding us*
> *with the body and blood of your Son Jesus Christ.*
> *Through him we offer you our souls and bodies*
> *to be a living sacrifice.*

Send us out
in the power of your Spirit
to live and work
to your praise and glory.
('Prayer after Communion'[1])

Lord Jesus, thank You for the cross and resurrection. Thank You for this meal of remembrance that You have given us. We pray that, having our identity in You, we will be empowered to walk righteously before You and all people. May we know Your presence with us and Your Holy Spirit in us. As we go out into a new week, may God, Father, Son and Holy Spirit, guard our hearts and minds to keep all our words and actions just, loving and true. Amen.

Feast of Unleavened Bread

Celebrate the Festival of Unleavened Bread, because it was on this very day that I brought your divisions out of Egypt. Celebrate this day as a lasting ordinance for the generations to come . . . For seven days no yeast is to be found in your houses . . . Eat nothing made with yeast. Wherever you live, you must eat unleavened bread. (Exod. 12:17, 19–20)

The communion service was instituted by Jesus during a Passover meal, with a backdrop of thanking God for salvation from slavery in the past, and a looking forward to the coming Messiah.

The Passover festival, which is also called the Feast of Unleavened Bread, commences on the fifteenth day of the Hebrew month of Nisan and lasts for either *seven* days (in Israel and for Reform Jews) or *eight* days (for Orthodox and most conservative Jews who live outside Israel). During this time, Jews will eat only food that contains no trace of yeast or other raising agent.

Leaven, or yeast, is a symbol for sin. The smallest trace of yeast affects the whole batch of dough in the same way as the smallest sin will spoil a life.

As a child in an Orthodox home, I can remember the great excitement and upheaval caused by the coming of Passover. On the day before Passover my mother would clean and scrub the whole kitchen: tables, shelves, cupboards, fridge, cooker— anything that might have been in contact with leaven. All the cutlery, crockery, kitchen utensils and cooking pots were stacked away in a cupboard and replaced with those used exclusively for Passover.

The night before Passover, my father would go round the house searching for leaven using a feather and a candle; we always left a piece of bread hidden so that he could find it. The following morning, the first day of Passover, this piece of bread was taken outside and burned with the words: 'If there is any other leaven in the house that we have missed, let it be as this piece of bread.' It was fun, but also very solemn. It was important that for the next seven days we ate only matzah and cakes made without raising agent.

In Hebrew, the word for leaven is *chometz,* meaning 'sour'. It is the nature of sin to make people sour. The Hebrew word *matzah* means 'sweet' or 'without sourness', and typifies the sweetness and wholesomeness of life without sin. It foreshadows the sinless, perfect life of Jesus.

For Jews, the putting away of all leaven symbolized breaking the old cycle of sin and starting afresh from Egypt to walk as a new nation before the Lord. They did not put away leaven in order to be redeemed, but because they had been redeemed.

In the Scriptures, leaven is used to describe the way sin can grow and spread throughout a person. Leaven passes secretly and silently through the mass of dough when bread is made. So it was with the doctrines of the Pharisees. Jesus spoke of false teaching and hypocrisy as leaven. He told his disciples, 'Be on your guard against the yeast of the Pharisees, which is hypocrisy' (Luke 12:1). And in 1 Corinthians 5:6–7a Paul tells the Corinthians who considered themselves to be in a healthy spiritual state: 'Your boasting is not good. Don't you know that a little yeast leavens the whole batch of dough? Get rid of the old yeast, so that you may be a new unleavened batch—as you really are.'

It was the unleavened Passover bread that Jesus broke and used as a symbol of His body. It is a picture of the perfection of Jesus, the Bread of Life, with not a trace of sin: 'Christ, our Passover lamb, has been sacrificed. Therefore let us keep the Festival, not with the old bread leavened with malice and wickedness, but with the unleavened bread of sincerity and truth' (1 Cor. 5:7b–8).

As we come to the communion table we remember that He gave His body as a perfect sinless sacrifice so that we can be saved.

So in our preparation, let us use this occasion to confess all known sin to God so that we come cleansed and renewed.

Prayer

> *God our Father,*
> *we come to you in sorrow for our sins.*
>
> *For turning away from you,*
> *and ignoring your will for our lives;*
> *Father, forgive us:*
> *save us and help us.*

For behaving just as we wish,
without thinking of you;
Father, forgive us:
save us and help us.

For failing you by what we do,
and think and say;
Father, forgive us:
save us and help us.

For living as if we were ashamed
to belong to your Son;
Father, forgive us:
save us and help us.
('Confession: Lament B50')[1]

Thoughts on
the bread

In temple times at Passover, the lamb was the last thing to be eaten, remembering the sacrifice that was necessary and the blood that was put on the lintels of the Israelite homes, protecting them from the angel of death.

In AD 70, as predicted by Jesus, Roman armies levelled the temple until only rubble and ashes remained, and the people of Israel were left without an altar and consequently unable to offer sacrifices. From this time, in the absence of the sacrificial lamb, an 'after-dish' of a piece of broken matzah, known as the *afikoman*, came into use at the Passover meal. The Passover bread came to represent the paschal lamb. The taste of the matzah and the reminder of the lamb were to linger in the memories of the descendants of Israel as the feast came to an end.

Yet, even before the temple was destroyed, Jesus used the *afikoman* (after-dish) to represent His own body. It seems He was looking forward to the time when the temple would be destroyed and Jews would use the *afikoman* to represent the paschal lamb.

In the making of the Passover bread, or matzah, the dough is crushed flat, then pierced with a pointed tool to prevent it rising in the oven. We remember Christ's body pierced with nails and a spear. For the Christian, this illustrates how Jesus was treated at His death: 'He was pierced for our transgressions, he was crushed for our iniquities' (Isa. 53:5).

In the Passover ceremony there are three pieces of matzah bread united in one container. For Jews this has various meanings. In my community it was taught that these signified the three castes of Jewish people: the *Cohanim* (direct descendants of Aaron), the Levites, and the rest of Israel. Other communities believe they represent the patriarchs Abraham, Isaac and Jacob, while others say they represent a unity of crowns: the crown of learning, the crown of priesthood and the crown of kingship. And Jews who have trusted in Jesus see them as representing the unity of the Godhead: Father, Son and Holy Spirit.

Early in the Seder (Passover) meal the middle piece of bread is broken, wrapped up and hidden; later in the meal this piece is brought out and shared by all. For Messianic Jews, this breaking and hiding of the middle matzah until the end of the meal takes on new significance as it was at this point during the Last Supper that Jesus said, 'This is my body, given [or 'broken'] for you' (Luke 22:19), using this as a picture of His death, burial and resurrection.

We understand the bread to represent to us the body of Jesus broken for us: the Lamb of God who takes away the sin of the world.

This is a solemn time as we remember both Jesus' physical suffering on the cross and His anguish as He bore the penalty of God for every one of our sins. But it is also a joyful time as we consider the redemption from sin planned from before the beginning of time and won for us at the cross. We rest in the undeserved love that Jesus has for each one of us, and our freedom to live in the light of the gospel.

Broken for me, broken for you,
The body of Jesus broken for you.

Come to My table and with Me dine;
Eat of My bread and drink of My wine.

This is My body given for you,
Eat it remembering I died for you.

This is My blood I shed for you,
For your forgiveness, making you new.
(Janet Lunt © 1978 Sovereign Music UK)

Now, as we look for His coming, we celebrate with this bread and wine, symbols of His one perfect sacrifice, proclaiming His death for our salvation and rejoicing in the power of His resurrection, until we share the fellowship of His kingdom.

Prayer

May we who share Christ's body live his risen life;
we who drink his cup bring life to others;
we whom the Spirit lights give light to the world.
Keep us firm in the hope you have set before us,
so we and all your children shall be free,
and the whole earth live to praise your name,
through Christ our Lord.
Amen.
('Prayer after Communion')[1]

Passover cups

As a child I remember Passover as a time when our drinking glasses were constantly being topped up, but we had to wait until we were told we could drink. Many times glasses got knocked over because of all the items on the table, and the wine spilt onto the book (Haggadah) that contained the readings and prayers. It was generally said that the Haggadah wasn't 'kosher' until it had wine stains on it!

In the liturgy of the Passover celebration a Jewish family will drink four cups during the course of the meal. These cups have names which are linked to the readings in the Seder celebration.

The first cup is drunk at the beginning of the Passover meal and is called the cup of *Sanctification*. It reminds Jews that they were set apart as a holy nation for special service to God.

The second cup is called the cup of *Instruction*. It is drunk as the narrative of the exodus is read, remembering the plagues God brought on Egypt. This cup is sometimes called the 'cup of plagues', while others know it as 'the cup of salvation' or 'the cup of wrath'.

The third cup focuses on God's action in 'buying back' His people and is called the cup of *Redemption*. This is drunk after the meal has been enjoyed.

The fourth cup is the cup of *Praise* and is drunk during the last section of the celebration, when psalms of praise are sung. 'I will lift up the cup of salvation and call on the name of the LORD' (Ps. 116:13).

The four cups represent the four expressions of deliverance

promised by God in Exodus 6:6–7: 'I will bring you out' from under the burdens of Egypt; 'I will free you' from slavery; 'I will redeem you' with an outstretched arm; and 'I will take you' as a nation. So to all Jews, these four cups represent different aspects of their historic deliverance from slavery in Egypt, one cup for each of God's sovereign acts against Pharaoh and the pagan gods. God's saving activity through Moses meant that they were no longer under the yoke of Egyptian tyranny.

Jewish people still remember God's redemption of the children of Israel from slavery when they drink the Passover cups. But at that Passover meal where Jesus instituted a new meaning for the celebration, His disciples saw that all along this was pointing to the One who would deliver us from the slavery of sin.

He was willing to die to bring about our deliverance. He became the sacrificial lamb foretold by Isaiah: 'and the LORD has laid on him the iniquity of us all' (Isa. 53:6).

And we who have put our trust in Him can know redemption from the slavery of sin.

As believers in Jesus we too have been set apart or *sanctified*—called to be holy as He is holy. We too need *instruction* so that we understand God's wrath on our sin and the punishment we deserve. We are able to rejoice in the knowledge that through Jesus we have *redemption*, and can *praise* Him for all that He has achieved through His death and resurrection.

We come today to take the bread and wine as reminders of

Christ's body broken and His blood shed for us. This theme of deliverance continues for us as Christians as we do so, and as we recall the spiritual redemption Jesus wrought for us. We have been redeemed and are no longer under the tyranny of sin!

Prayer

It is right to give him thanks and praise . . .
it is our duty and our joy,
at all times and in all places
to give you thanks and praise,
holy Father, heavenly King,
almighty and eternal God,
through Jesus Christ your only Son our Lord.[1]

And now we give you thanks
because Christ our paschal sacrifice
has made us children of the light,
rising to new and everlasting life.
He has opened the gates of heaven
to receive his faithful people.
His death is our ransom from death,
his resurrection is our rising to life.
The joy of the resurrection renews the whole world,
while choirs of heaven sing for ever to your glory.
('Prayers at the Preparation of the Table')[2]

The second cup—
'Take this cup
from me!'

Father, if you are willing, take this cup from me; yet
not my will, but yours be done. (Luke 22:42)

Since the days of Moses the Jewish nation knew that sin had
to be punished either in the person who had sinned or in a
substitute. They understood that the death of an animal was
necessary for the atonement of their sins. The prophets taught
that one day God would send one final Lamb in the place of the
many lambs. Isaiah made this clear, yet to this day the people
of Israel don't recognize the Lamb who came as the perfect
sacrifice for sin.

He was pierced for our transgressions,
   he was crushed for our iniquities;
the punishment that brought us peace was on him,
   and by his wounds we are healed.
We all, like sheep, have gone astray,
   each of us has turned to our own way;
and the LORD has laid on him
   the iniquity of us all.
He was oppressed and afflicted,
   yet he did not open his mouth;
he was led like a lamb to the slaughter,
   and as a sheep before its shearers is silent,
   so he did not open his mouth. (Isa. 53:5–7)

In the garden of Gethsemane the Lord Jesus prayed that the
cup of God's judgement on sin might be taken from Him. He
knew what lay ahead—beating, humiliation and death on a
cross. That was bad enough, but worst of all, He knew He

had to drink the cup of God's wrath against sin. We will never know what that cost Him.

The second cup, the 'cup of instruction', that Jews drink at Passover is sometimes known by Messianic Jews as 'the cup of wrath', and when they celebrate Passover it is their tradition not to drink this cup in recognition that Jesus the Messiah drank it in our place.

This cup is also called the 'cup of plagues' as Jews retell the account of the dreadful plagues that God brought on Egypt because of Pharaoh's unwillingness to let His people go.

In Jewish tradition a full cup is a symbol of joy. As Jewish people we do not rejoice that our enemies had to suffer plagues and die in order for us to be set free, so during the Seder meal we make the cup less full by removing a drop of wine from our cup for each of the ten plagues as we recite them: blood, frogs, lice, wild beasts, pestilence, boils, hail, locusts, darkness, slaying of the firstborn. This is a solemn part of the Passover meal.

At the Last Supper Jesus was looking ahead to the following day when He would drink the cup of God's wrath in order to redeem you and me. We have all sinned, we all deserve judgement and punishment, but He has taken that cup of judgement on Himself so that we can be set free!

> Yes, finished! the Messiah dies,
>
> Cut off for sins, but not His own;
>
> completed is the sacrifice,
>
> The great redeeming work is done.

Yes, finished! all the debt is paid,
Justice divine is satisfied,
The grand and full atonement made;
God for a guilty world has died!
(Charles Wesley; Praise Trust, 2000)

God's judgement on the last day on me—and I trust on you—will read 'Justified' (made right). How is this possible for us? Only because of Jesus' death, and only when we have acknowledged that our crimes were punished in Christ on the cross. Then, praise God, our sins are forgiven, to be remembered no more; and we are counted among the 'righteous'.

Prayer

Lord God, as we rise from this table once again, we thank You for the reminder that the Lord Jesus Christ walked the way of the cross in humble obedience to Your will and purpose. We pray that, as we go out into the world this week with all its trials and temptations, You would help us to walk also in faith and obedience to You, rejoicing in Your greatness and power, Your love, gentleness and mercy. Enable us by Your Spirit to honour You with every thought, word and action, and make us a blessing to all with whom we come into contact. Amen.

The third cup—'in remembrance of me'

This cup is the new covenant in my blood; do this, whenever you drink it, in remembrance of me.

(1 Cor. 11:25)

Have you ever heard a message that changed your understanding in a totally new way? A fresh vision of God's truth that blew you away as each implication sank in?

Perhaps you can look back to early in your Christian life when the gospel message and the possibility of a relationship with Jesus were new. But as we get older we don't often get fresh revelations like that, and certainly God doesn't give completely new truths now that the Bible is complete.

At the Last Supper recorded in Luke's Gospel, when Jesus celebrated Passover with his disciples, a revolutionary new revelation was given. The full significance was perhaps lost on the disciples until later, but it was still a radical and shocking truth. The disciples had just heard the words of the Passover, as familiar to them as the 1 Corinthians passage is to us. Then Jesus took the bread and explained a new meaning. What He was saying was that, until that point, when they broke the bread it had been to remember the 'bread of affliction' which their fathers ate in Egypt. But from now on, it should remind them of *His* body which would be broken for them on the following day.

When He took the wine after supper—the third cup, known in the Passover as the cup called 'Redemption', he was effectively saying, 'Before, when you lifted this cup, you remembered Almighty God who broke the power of slavery and redeemed you as a nation, and you were grateful. But from now on, whenever you do these things, remember the redemption that I am going to win for you with My blood—a redemption from a greater bondage, that of sin and guilt.'

When Jesus poured this cup He said it was the cup of the new covenant between God and man, sealed in His blood. As often as we drink it, we are to do it in remembrance of Him. In short, He was saying, 'Don't do this in remembrance of Egypt—do it in remembrance of *Me*.'

For us as twenty-first-century Christians, the words we read are not new, but it may help our meditation if we change the emphasis from 'in remembrance' to '*of me*'.

What do you think about when you hold the bread and the wine? Clearly we focus on Christ, the price He paid, the salvation He won and the suffering it cost Him. But Jesus said, 'Remember Me.'

When a loved one dies, our grief is focused on the loss of that person, but after a while we remember them as they were—alive. In the same way, when we come to communion, we should remember not only Christ's death, but all we can of Jesus:

- His love for sinners (the woman caught in adultery)
- His teaching (the Sermon on the Mount)
- His power (stilling the storm)
- His love of children ('let them come to Me')
- His glory (the transfiguration)
- His humility (washing His disciples' feet)

• His love (while we were sinners He died for us).

> Behold the Lamb who bears our sins away,
> Slain for us: and we remember
> The promise made that all who come in faith
> Find forgiveness at the cross.
> (Stuart Townend, Keith & Kristyn
> Getty © 2007 Thankyou Music)

We who know the Lord Jesus personally and know ourselves forgiven of our wickedness take up both the bread and the cup of redemption in Jesus' blood with enormous gratitude.

Prayer

Thank You that as we approach this communion meal we can remember You, Lord Jesus. We thank You for being willing to enter our world as a helpless baby. We remember Your perfect life and every example of Your humility, grace and power. We praise You for the wonder of Your mighty, dying love and the promise of eternal life that we have because of Your victory over sin and death. Amen.

The new covenant between God and His people

At the Last Supper Jesus gave a radical new teaching when they came to the end of the meal and poured the third cup. He said: '*This* cup is the new covenant in my blood', switching the focus from the redemption from Egypt to the redemption that is offered through His blood.

The disciples were familiar with the old covenant. Unlike most contracts, this covenant was not so much an agreement between two or more parties but a set of conditions initiated by God. Israel had no say in determining the framework of the covenant. God defined all of the conditions, duties and obligations of the covenant, and the people could only accept or reject God's offer. It is obvious why this was the case: God is the Creator, and we are His creation.

The people's acceptance of those conditions cemented their relationship with God. But their later disobedience cut them off from the blessings God had promised.

One of the earliest covenants was made after the flood recorded in Genesis. We are told that when Noah came out of the ark he built an altar and took animals and birds as a burnt offering to God, who made a covenant that He would never again flood the earth. 'When the LORD smelt the pleasing aroma, the LORD said in his heart, "I will never again . . . strike down every living creature as I have done . . . I have set my bow in the cloud, and it shall be a sign of the covenant between me and the earth . . . When the bow is in the clouds I will see it and remember the everlasting covenant"' (Gen. 8:21; 9:13, 16, ESV).

Many of the covenants in the Bible were sealed with blood.

This is seen after Moses had instructed the children of Israel in the law given to him on Mount Sinai, as explained in Hebrews:

> When Moses had proclaimed every command of the law to all the people, he took the blood of calves . . . and sprinkled the scroll and all the people. He said, 'This is the blood of the covenant, which God has commanded you to keep.' . . . In fact, the law requires that nearly everything be cleansed with blood, and without the shedding of blood there is no forgiveness. (Heb. 9:19–22)

Under the old covenant, the death of an animal was necessary to atone for the sins of Israel, but this had to be offered regularly and it was a temporary covenant, mirroring something better to come. This is what Jesus was stating when He spoke those words at the Last Supper—'This cup is the new covenant in my blood.'

The new covenant Jesus was talking about was the perfect and permanent sacrifice made when He died in our place. This takes God's people from the bondage of the law to the freedom that comes through grace. He lives today to save, redeeming us from sin, the Lamb of God, broken for us, bringing in the new covenant in His blood. Glory to His name!

As we trace God's covenant faithfulness to His people, it is amazing to realize that He would often give them signs to serve as reminders not just for them, but also for Him! As the rainbow in the sky reminds Him of His promise not to flood the earth again, so the bread and wine remind Him of His promise.

As we gather to proclaim Christ's death as a memorial before God, He sees the signs and blesses us, nourishing our faith with His body and blood by the Holy Spirit. He remembers His promises to us that, as we trust in Jesus, He will free us from the bondage of sin through His shed blood.

In communion, God remembers, and we receive.

Prayer

> *So, Father, as we remember all that Jesus did,*
> *in him we plead with confidence his sacrifice*
> *made once for all upon the cross.*
> *Bringing before you the bread of life and cup of salvation,*
> *we proclaim his death and resurrection*
> *until he comes in glory.*[1]

Heavenly Father, nourish our souls by Your Holy Spirit, as You have promised. Amen.

The Messiah
has come!

The Messianic hope is stronger at Passover than at any other time in the Jewish calendar. Passover is held in the month of Nisan, the month when Israel was redeemed from Egypt, and Jews believe it will be in Nisan that Israel will once more be redeemed. Jewish people not only look back with thankfulness for salvation from slavery, but they also look forward to the coming Messiah.

It is traditional at a Jewish Passover celebration meal for a place to be set for the prophet Elijah. There are two reasons for this.

The first reason is that Jews expected—and some still expect—the Messiah to reveal himself at Passover and that Elijah would appear first to 'prepare the way' for the coming King. He would restore the borders of Israel to those promised by Abraham; he would restore the ten lost tribes; and he would bring in the Messianic era of peace and righteousness. There is a moment in the Seder when Elijah's cup is filled to the brim with wine and the front door is opened to let him in. The tradition is that, at this time, the prophet Elijah is expected to arrive, and the person who opens the door is supposed to welcome him to the feast with the Hebrew words *baruch haba*: 'Blessed is he who comes', or more colloquially, 'Welcome!' This is followed by a moment of 'fun' as the children check to see if the level of wine in Elijah's cup has gone down.

Some say that this ceremony is also performed so that those who believe the 'blood libel' (that Jews sacrifice a Gentile child at Passover) can see the Jews have nothing to hide.

Secondly, the laying of a place for Elijah is a symbol of hospitality for a wayfarer. No one should be left out at the Passover meal, and often people who would otherwise be alone are invited to join in with a family's celebration.

As those who follow Jesus, we know that the Messiah has already come. So what of Elijah? In Matthew 17 Jesus suggests that John the Baptist is Elijah. The disciples ask Jesus, 'Why . . . do the teachers of the law say that Elijah must come first?' Jesus replies, '"I tell you, Elijah has already come, and they did not recognise him . . ." Then the disciples understood that he was talking to them about John the Baptist' (Matt. 17:10, 12–13).

The Bible is clear that John the Baptist is called 'Elijah' because he came in the 'spirit and power of Elijah' (Luke 1:17), not because he was Elijah in a literal sense. John the Baptist is the New Testament forerunner who points the way to the arrival of the Lord.

As we celebrate communion we remember that Jesus—our Messiah and Saviour—has already come. We remember that God's wrath was poured out on Him for the sake of those—including us—who did not acknowledge Him. While we were sinners, Christ died for us. We break bread and drink the cup in remembrance of Him. And as we solemnly remember His sacrifice for us, we also contemplate with joy His return to usher in the true Messianic age.

Prayer

Take us out into the world to do your will, to bring glory to

Your name and to commend Christ to all; until that day when You come or call and we take our place at that eternal banquet, where we will need no symbols to remind us of You. For there You will be our light, our joy and our eternal bliss. Amen.

Easter
firstfruits

If Christ has not been raised, your faith is futile; you are
still in your sins. Then those also who have fallen asleep
in Christ are lost. If only for this life we have hope in
Christ, we are of all people most to be pitied. But Christ
has indeed been raised from the dead, the firstfruits
of those who have fallen asleep . . . For as in Adam all
die, so in Christ all will be made alive. But each in turn:
Christ, the firstfruits; then, when he comes, those who
belong to him. (1 Cor. 15:17–20, 22–23)

Almost all the early Christians were Jewish and they
celebrated the resurrection of Jesus at Passover. After
the Council of Nicaea, the date of Easter was calculated from
the solar calendar rather than from the Jewish lunar calendar,
diminishing the connection between the two festivals.

As Easter people we celebrate the day of firstfruits
whenever we come to the communion table and especially
on Resurrection Sunday, and Paul's words in 1 Corinthians
15 are very familiar to us. But if we see them only in the
New Testament context we miss some of the wonder and
significance of this event.

The Gospels are clear that Jesus rose on the first day of
the week immediately following the start of Passover. In the
Jewish calendar this day marks the Jewish festival called Yom
HaBikkurim, or 'the day of firstfruits', as the Lord instructed
Moses to tell the Israelites in Leviticus:

Speak to the Israelites and say to them: 'When you
enter the land I am going to give you and you reap its

harvest, bring to the priest a sheaf of the first grain you harvest. He is to wave the sheaf before the LORD so it will be accepted on your behalf . . . you must sacrifice as a burnt offering to the LORD a lamb a year old without defect, together with its grain offering . . . a food offering presented to the LORD, a pleasing aroma . . . Count fifty days up to the day after the seventh Sabbath, and then present an offering of new grain to the LORD.' (Lev. 23:9–13, 16)

The offering of the firstfruits is a ceremony which commences the marking off of the fifty days to the feast of firstfruits of the wheat harvest, which is called Shavuot, or Pentecost. Yom HaBikkurim celebrates the beginning of the barley harvest and its theme is new life, or life from the dead.

And what happened on Yom HaBikkurim, the day of firstfruits, on the first day of the week following the crucifixion? Jesus rose from the dead! No wonder Paul calls Him the firstfruits of the resurrection.

But not only did Jesus rise from the dead on that day, He also gave the Father His own firstfruits offering by opening the graves so that dead people were seen alive in Jerusalem. The resurrection of Jesus points to the rising from the dead of 'those . . . who have fallen asleep in Christ' (1 Cor. 15:18). He is the Firstfruits, pointing to our resurrection and the grounds and foundation of our hope in Christ. 'Christ, the firstfruits; then, when he comes, those who belong to him' (15:23).

Christ once raised from the dead dies no more:

death has no more dominion over him.
In dying he died to sin once for all:
in living he lives to God.
See yourselves therefore as dead to sin:
and alive to God in Jesus Christ our Lord.

Christ has been raised from the dead:
the first fruits of those who sleep . . .
for as in Adam all die:
even so in Christ shall all be made alive.
('Easter Anthems')[1]

We come today to celebrate around His table the death and resurrection of Jesus our Saviour. This was not a random act whereby God turned a tragedy into a triumph. It was an event carefully planned from the beginning of time that can be traced throughout the pages of Scripture.

Easter is the feast of freedom in which the resurrected Christ sits at the table with His disciples. It is the eating and drinking in the kingdom of God which the Resurrected One anticipates with everyone whom He has made a friend.

Let us celebrate the feast!

Prayer

Man of heaven, born to earth
To restore us to your heaven
Here we bow in awe beneath
Your searching eyes
From your tears comes our joy

From your death our life shall spring
By your resurrection power we shall rise

We worship at your feet
Where wrath and mercy meet
And a guilty world is washed
By love's pure stream
For us he was made sin
Oh, help me take it in . . .
I worship, I worship
The Lamb who was slain.
(Graham Kendrick, 'Come and See'
© 1989 Make Way Music)

Easter eggs

Passover and Easter are both holidays that involve eggs in some form. The first records of eating Passover eggs and of giving eggs as presents at Easter go back to medieval Germany. Could the use of eggs by adherents of the two faith groups have a common origin?

Every Passover, Jews place a roasted or burnt hard-boiled egg on the Passover ceremonial plate, and the celebrants also eat hard-boiled eggs dipped in salt water as part of the ceremony.

Although eggs are not mentioned at all in the account of the exodus, the egg has become a prominent symbol for Passover, as indicated by its place on the Seder plate. It is not specifically mentioned in the Haggadah, and no one really knows when the egg became a part of Passover. It most likely was introduced after the Second Temple period as a reminder of the freewill offerings made in temple worship.

In Jewish thinking, the rounded shape of an egg symbolizes the cycle of life and the egg is seen to represent new life and hope, and triumph over death. The egg is completely smooth and has no opening. It is thus compared to the mourner who bears his or her grief in silence and therefore appears composed and unaffected on the surface. For Jews, eggs are the traditional food of mourning and are the first food served to mourners after they return from a funeral.

So it is thought that the eggs at Passover symbolize mourning for two events: the tears that were shed by their forefathers in captivity in Egypt, and the sorrow at the destruction of the temple in Jerusalem. The burnt egg is also seen as a symbolic representation of the sacrifices which ceased with the destruction of the temple by the Romans in AD 70.

'As the feast of Easter developed in Christian tradition, so did the festival's preparatory period, known as Lent. This involved fasting and later abstinence from certain foods, including eggs . . . By the time of the medieval theologian Thomas Aquinas (c.1225–74), eggs, milk and meat were all forbidden during Lent', for 'they originate from animals that provide us with flesh'.[1] This established the tradition of Pancake Day on Shrove Tuesday to mark the last consumption of eggs and dairy before Ash Wednesday, when Lent begins.

'In pre-refrigeration days, it would be difficult to preserve milk and meat products until Easter, but the same was not true of eggs',[2] which could be hard-boiled and kept until the end of the fasting period.

Since hens still lay eggs during Lent but those eggs couldn't be eaten until Easter Sunday, some people may have thought that decorating them was a good idea—the Easter egg was born! Some people still dye and paint chicken eggs, but a modern custom has substituted these with the chocolate eggs we enjoy today.

These eggs came to symbolize the empty tomb of Jesus, from which He rose again. 'One ancient tradition was the staining of Easter eggs with the colour red "in memory of the blood of Christ"' shed on the cross,[3] and in 1610 'the Christian Church officially adopted the custom, regarding the eggs as a symbol of the resurrection of Jesus',[4] linking the cracking open of the eggs with the empty tomb of Jesus.

So, for both Jew and Christian, eggs have great symbolism, and at Easter it is good to remind ourselves of these origins. But for us, as we come to the table of the Lord, we have the bread and wine: symbols of the body and blood of our Saviour.

This Easter time, although we mourn over the necessity of Jesus' death, we rejoice that Jesus broke open the grave and rose from the dead to secure victory over sin and the grave.

Prayer

Thank You, Lord Jesus, that death could not hold You. We rejoice to know that, because of Your resurrection, we too can live. The sting of sin and death has been removed and You have won the victory for us. Thank You that the grave is the doorway into Your presence. Thank You that we can live in the power of Your resurrection until that day comes. Amen.

In an unworthy manner?

Whenever you eat this bread and drink this cup, you proclaim the Lord's death until he comes. So then, whoever eats the bread or drinks the cup of the Lord in an unworthy manner will be guilty of sinning against the body and blood of the Lord. Everyone ought to examine themselves before they eat of the bread and drink from the cup. For those who eat and drink without discerning the body of Christ eat and drink judgment on themselves. (1 Cor. 11:26–29)

It is a joy to meet together as brothers and sisters to remember the death of our Saviour. But it's sad when some who are invited to the table don't eat. I have heard it said that they don't feel worthy; that these verses in 1 Corinthians 11 make them hesitate.

What does the Bible mean when it talks about eating and drinking 'in an unworthy manner'? I believe there are only three things we should consider that would prevent us taking part.

Firstly, we shouldn't eat the bread or drink from the cup if *we don't believe* that Jesus died for us. When we come together we are proclaiming that the death of Jesus was an all-surpassing act of sacrifice for our sin that makes us free and gives us life. This sacrifice is the foundation of our hope and our source of joy. If we cannot proclaim this to be true for us, then we shouldn't eat or drink here. But if you have never asked Jesus for forgiveness, now is the time. He is more willing to forgive you than you are to confess. You could receive new life and communion today.

Secondly, we shouldn't partake if *we are out of fellowship with God*. Even as Christians we can wilfully reject the grace of God by deliberate sins, saying to ourselves, 'I know what I'm doing is wrong, but I'm going to continue doing it.' This is different from the awareness of our sin that drives us to Jesus. If you are a Christian and you need to put things right with God, you can also do that right now, and then draw near to our Creator and Redeemer, knowing you are accepted and loved.

Thirdly, we shouldn't eat or drink if *we are out of fellowship with another Christian*. Breaking bread together unites us in a powerful way. We struggle to enjoy a meal with someone if we are in disagreement with them or annoyed with them. This is even more true around the table with Christ at the head.

According to the rabbis, on the Day of Atonement (Yom Kippur), the works of 'prayer, penitence and charity' will atone for sins committed against God. But the rabbis teach that these works will not atone for sins against our neighbours unless and until we have first gone to our neighbours and righted the wrongs committed.

The greatest Rabbi of all, in His Sermon on the Mount, made this very clear: 'if you are offering your gift at the altar and there remember that your brother or sister has something against you, leave your gift there in front of the altar. First go and be reconciled to them; then come and offer your gift' (Matt. 5:23–24). If this was true of the altar in the temple, how much more is it true when we come to the table of the Lord.

Jesus showed the link between our relationship with God and our relationship with our neighbour when he taught His disciples to pray: 'Forgive us our sins, for we also forgive everyone who sins against us' (Luke 11:4).

We cannot have real communion with Christ if we have no communion with our brother or sister. Although we are still in union with Jesus because we have been accepted through His blood, we may be out of communion with Him. If you need to put things right with another Christian, then it will be best for you to wait until next time to take communion.

Because salvation is free and all of God's grace, He invites us to this table. He gives *all* those who believe in the power of the cross and in the sacrifice Jesus made for us *the right* to come. We weren't perfect when we were saved, we aren't perfect now, and we don't have to be perfect to sit at this table with Christ. We don't have salvation by grace and communion by works. Remember the accusation that the Pharisees made when Jesus sat with Levi the tax collector: that He ate 'with . . . sinners' (Matt. 9:11).

If you are trusting Jesus as your Saviour, come and take part. It is Jesus who invites you. Don't wait to be good enough. You are already counted as righteous.

When we come to the communion service we are reminded that He is the Host; it is He who invites us to His table.

Prayer

> Come, Lord Jesus, be our guest,
> stay with us for day is ending.
> With friend, with stranger,
> with young and with old,
> be among us tonight.
> Come close to us that we may come close to you.
> Forgive us that we may forgive one another.
> Renew us so that, where we have failed,
> we may begin again. Amen.[1]

May we who eat this bread live a life worthy of the name Christian.

May we who drink the cup bring life to others.

May we by life and speech reveal Christ and bring gospel light into the places where we walk each day.

Amen.

In an unworthy manner?

Tishah
B'av

Av is the fifth month in the Hebrew calendar, falling in July or August of the Western calendar. The ninth day of Av is the annual fast day in Judaism, called the festival of Tishah B'Av. On this day Jews remember the saddest day in the Jewish calendar. It is a day full of mourning to remember that on this date there were a number of disasters in Jewish history.

Primarily it is the date of the destruction of both the first temple by the Babylonians and the second temple by the Romans in Jerusalem. Both occurred on the ninth of the Hebrew month of Av, but about 655 years apart.

Over time, Tishah B'Av came to be a Jewish day of mourning not only for these events, but also for later tragedies. The expulsion of Jews from England in 1290, from France in 1306 and from Spain in 1492 also occurred in the month of Av. And more recently, it was the ninth day of Av in 1941 when the German SS commander Heinrich Himmler and the Nazi Party approved 'the Final Solution'—the Holocaust, which led to the destruction of six million Jews, almost one-third of the world's Jewish population.

So all observant Jews will hold a twenty-five-hour fast at this time. There is no finery in the synagogue; the embroidered hangings in front of the ark and the bright ornate coverings for the scrolls are changed to very plain ones. To this day there are no musical instruments used in synagogues. The book of Lamentations, which mourns the destruction of Jerusalem, is read in the synagogue, followed by the recitation of liturgical dirges that lament the loss of the temples and Jerusalem.

Why am I telling you this as we come around the communion table? It is because I want to encourage you that God is faithful to His promises. Listen to the words of the prophet Zechariah, whose name means 'God remembered' and who lived in exile after the fall of Jerusalem: 'The word of the LORD Almighty came to me. This is what the LORD Almighty says: "The fasts of the fourth, fifth, seventh and tenth months will become joyful and glad occasions and happy festivals for Judah. Therefore love truth and peace"' (Zech. 8:18–19).

The book of Zechariah focuses on the return from exile and the rebuilding of the temple, and promises that God will turn their fasting into feasting. Zechariah also talks about the coming of the Messiah: 'Rejoice greatly, Daughter Zion! Shout, Daughter Jerusalem! See, your king comes to you, righteous and victorious, lowly and riding on a donkey, on a colt, the foal of a donkey' (Zech. 9:9).

While at this time of year Jews remember the destruction of the temple buildings, it is fitting that we gather to remember the One who said, 'Destroy this temple, and I will raise it again in three days' (John 2:19). He was not, of course, talking about the building, but of His body.

Jesus fulfilled that promise and in doing so fulfilled the prophecy of Zechariah. Our King-Messiah has commanded us to feast as we remember Him. His death was God's way of bringing reconciliation between God and man.

Since his triumph over death Jesus has become our temple; more than that, He is also our High Priest, a priest not in the line of Aaron, but of the order of Melchizedek. Further still, He has become our atonement, our sacrifice for sin. All who trust in Him know their sins are covered and atoned for.

In God's sovereignty the buildings of the second temple were again destroyed, this time by the Romans. He also allowed the building of a mosque on the site of the temple. This was to underline the fact that no more sacrifice was needed or would be accepted after the one final perfect sacrifice of His Son.

The temple of Jesus' body was destroyed and rose again in victory. He paid the price of our peace with His body and blood.

Now the temple of God is with men as Christ dwells in us by the Holy Spirit.

Prayer

Dear Lord, at this time of mourning for the Jewish people, we are full of thanks that no evil power can thwart Your sovereign plan to build Your kingdom. As we look forward to that day when our King comes again, when peace is proclaimed to the nations, when His rule extends from the river to the ends of the earth, we proclaim You our Messiah and coming King. We exalt Your name and pray that our lives will bring You all the honour due to Your holy name. Amen.

Purim

Iran is home to one of the world's oldest civilizations. It has a history of conflict with the surrounding nations, and particularly with ancient Israel. Today Iran is developing nuclear weapons with the capability of reaching the modern state of Israel.

Around 2,500 years ago the situation was very similar. Iran—or Persia, as it was then known—posed a huge threat to the future of the Jewish people when Haman the Agagite plotted their destruction. We read about this in the book of Esther.

During March in the Western calendar, Jews around the world celebrate the festival of Purim. The word 'Purim' means 'Lots', a reminder that Haman cast lots to decide on the best date to kill the Jewish people. The festival is a time of great celebration to remember how God used a series of unlikely events and a young Jewish girl called Esther, who became queen to King Ahasuerus, to accomplish the protection of the whole nation.

I remember Purim being a fun festival when I was a child. In the celebrations within the Jewish community, people go to their friends' houses with a plate of sweets and cakes to exchange. On this plate there are little three-cornered pastries called *Hamantaschen*, meaning 'Haman's pockets'. Some will dress up as Esther, Mordecai or Haman, and whilst drunkenness is frowned on in Jewish culture, at this one festival Jews are allowed to get drunk. Tradition has it that they can get so drunk that they cannot tell the difference between 'Blessed be Mordecai' and 'Cursed be Haman'.

We would gather in the synagogue where the whole book of Esther would be read to the congregation. Normally the synagogue services are solemn occasions when the books of the law are read, but at Purim the atmosphere is quite different. As the story of Esther is read, the congregation will stamp their feet or wave football rattles or similar objects whenever the name 'Haman' is said, in order to drown out the sound of his name.

In many ways Queen Esther had similar qualities to the Lord Jesus. She left a loving home to live with strangers and was submissive to earthly authorities. She spent time in prayer and fasting before a critical moment. Then she went into the presence of the king and interceded for her people, pleading for them at the risk of her own life. She said, 'How can I bear to see disaster fall on my people? How can I bear to see the destruction of my family?' (Esth. 8:6). And she achieved a great salvation.

This was the same sentiment that would lead Christ to sacrifice Himself for us. But how much greater were the humility and condescension of Jesus who, though He was God, submitted Himself to live amongst those He had made. He submitted to their corrupt authorities and finally to their unjust execution. Much more, He became sin for us and took our punishment.

[Jesus Christ], being in very nature God,

did not consider equality with God something to be
used to his own advantage;
rather, he made himself nothing
by taking the very nature of a servant,
being made in human likeness.
And being found in appearance as a man,
he humbled himself
by becoming obedient to death—
even death on a cross! (Phil. 2:6–8)

Christ gave His life for us so that we might be redeemed. Because of His sacrifice we will one day share in His resurrection. And He lives to make intercession for us so that we will have the ability to resist temptation and depend on the atonement for our eternal salvation.

Prayer

Lord Jesus Christ, Your life was taken from You by wickedness;

Evil thought it had triumphed, but You rose again in power and in might.

Our lives were dead in sinfulness until we gave them up to You and lived.

You have translated us from darkness into light, but the task is not complete.

Take us, Lord, bend us, reshape us in Your image.

Make us the people we were meant to be.

Guide us, Lord, day by day, and may the knowledge of

Your love and mercy lead us into lives of faith and acts of service, bringing glory to Your holy name. Amen.

Good
Friday

Usually, when we come to the communion table, we think of the Last Supper. We share the bread and wine and remember with immense gratitude Christ's sacrifice for us.

But today is Good Friday, and the events of the Thursday and Friday before that first Easter involved much more than the Passover meal. That was just the start.

At the Passover meal there is a point where the participants wash their hands. This is not primarily for hygiene purposes as none of them would have come to the table without first washing their hands. Rather it is a ritualistic hand-washing to indicate the need for purity as they come to celebrate this holy feast. It is a symbolic expression of washing away impurity. In my home it was the custom for members to wash one another's hands. A bowl, a towel and a jug of water are passed around the table, and each person will pour water onto the hands of the person next to them.

In the account of the Last Supper we read that Jesus got up from the meal, took off his outer clothing, wrapped a towel around His waist and poured water into a basin. Then, instead of washing their hands, He began to wash His disciples' feet, drying them with the towel that was wrapped around Him.

After He had done this, He resumed His place at the table and said, 'Do you understand what I have done for you? . . . You call me "Teacher" and "Lord", and rightly so, for that is what I am. Now that I, your Lord and Teacher, have washed your feet, you also should wash one another's feet' (John 13:12–14).

As Jesus took the bread and the wine, which to the disciples were symbolic of the escape from Egypt, He spoke of His body being broken and His blood spilt. He talked of one who would betray Him, and about them being clean. It must have been a very confusing occasion, and sadly, despite all that Jesus had told them in advance about His betrayal and death, they didn't understand, and it came as a dreadful shock to them when their Master was arrested. They all fled into the dark as Jesus was taken and tried by an illegal meeting of the Sanhedrin.

We read that Peter followed at a distance but, as Jesus had predicted would happen, he denied knowing Him. Despite all his protestations of loyalty, Peter failed his Lord.

The next morning, the pretence of the judicial process continued.

Jesus is hauled before Pilate. The governor finds no fault in Him and, because He is a Galilean, passes him over to Herod, the puppet king. Herod, totally incompetent, soon tires of Jesus. The prisoner is very poor sport. He won't answer questions and doesn't beg for mercy even when roughed up, so Herod sends Him back to Pilate.

The pressure is on Pilate. The Passover, which is a celebration about freedom, has just begun. Pilate feared the crowds and, in desperation to get the situation sorted out, he passes the crucifixion order and Jesus is condemned.

This was the darkest time. Even the sun hid its light. For three hours there was darkness. The earth itself was startled and filled with dread and wonder. A man was dying, but he was no ordinary man. The Creator had become sin for the creature. He was taking their punishment. God was separated from God for that period.

Then that loud triumphant cry, 'It is finished!' The price had been paid—in full!

We don't enter into the despair of the disciples at the death and burial of Jesus. We have the understanding of why these events occurred and we live in the light of the resurrection. For us, the events of Good Friday fill us with gratitude and hope.

All the disciples forsook Jesus and fled, Peter had betrayed Jesus, and they were far from being those who would follow in the steps of the Master and show the same sacrificial love in washing one another's feet. But Jesus had known this would happen, and He loved them just the same. And how graciously He restored the relationship with His disciples after He rose again.

How often we fail our Lord! We admit that we are far from being the people we should be. We let Him down and betray His trust on a regular basis. But this table is a place for saved sinners. Jesus can wash us clean and make us pure before God. He invites to His table all who love Him, who honestly repent of their sin, and who seek to live in peace and humility with one another. What a Saviour!

Prayer

Lord I lift your name on high
Lord I love to sing your praises . . .

You came from heaven to earth
To show the way
From the earth to the cross
My debt to pay
From the cross to the grave
From the grave to the sky
Lord I lift your name on high.
(Rick Founds © 1989 Maranatha! Music)

Go forth in peace, with the love of God in your hearts, the Word of God on your lips, and the wonder of Easter in your minds. May the resurrection power of Jesus be in your every sinew, to live a life worthy of your calling.

Tu B'Shevat: 'New Year for Trees'

On the fifteenth day of the Hebrew month of Shevat (around February), Jewish people celebrate a minor festival known as Tu B'Shevat. It is also known as the 'New Year for Trees'.

In the UK this is a fairly dismal time of year for trees and flowers. There are a few snowdrops and crocuses giving us promise of spring, but almost all the trees remain bare. In Israel, however, this time of year marks the end of the winter rains. Tradition has it that on this day, at God's command, the sap begins to rise in trees. There, new life will soon appear in what has looked dry and lifeless all winter.

The origin of this festival is found in Leviticus 19:23–24 and God's instructions through Moses that fruit from trees was not to be eaten during their first three years; the fourth year's fruit was for God; and only after that could the people of Israel eat the fruit.

In contemporary Israel, the day is celebrated as an ecological awareness day that reminds Jewish people of our connection to the earth and our role as caretakers of the environment. Trees are planted in celebration. Schoolchildren will go out planting saplings on the hillsides and valleys of Israel, while Jewish children in the West go round collecting money to pay for these trees.

Knowingly or unknowingly, they are bringing to life the words of Isaiah 35:1: 'The desert and the parched land will be glad; the wilderness will rejoice and blossom. Like the crocus, it will burst into bloom; it will rejoice greatly and shout for joy.'

The annual miracle of the signs of life returning to woods and gardens reminds us of the two miracles of the crucifixion. Firstly, Christ, though dead and buried, rose again in new life and power, and now lives to make intercession for us. And secondly, that death and resurrection bring new life to all who believe—those who once were dead in sin. Until the Holy Spirit moved in our lives, giving us faith, we were spiritually lifeless, dead in our sins. Then we received new life, spiritual life, and (hopefully) the change was as obvious as the flush of new leaves on a tree.

The change of seasons also reminds us that God is faithful to His promises. As we can be confident that 'seedtime and harvest, cold and heat . . . will never cease' (Gen. 8:22), so too we can be confident in Jesus' promise of His return.

> Raised with Him to endless life
> He will hold me fast
> Till our faith is turned to sight
> When He comes at last.
> (Matthew Merker, 'He Will Hold Me Fast' © 2013
> Getty Music [BMI]/Matthew Merker Music [BMI])

As we come to the Lord's table to remember Christ's death and resurrection, we remember that He died as the atoning sacrifice for our sin, but now lives; that He is the firstfruits of resurrection and that there is life for us after we pass the portal of death. We don't know when the Lord Jesus Christ will return, but, with the writer to the Hebrews, we can confidently say, 'In just a little while, he who is coming will come and will not delay' (Heb. 10:37).

When we take the bread and wine, the symbols of Jesus' broken body and shed blood, let us rejoice in the new life we have in Jesus because of all He did for us on that wooden cross two thousand years ago. May we be encouraged that the endless life Jesus died to win is ours; and if He comes before He calls us home to heaven, we will witness that glorious return.

Prayer

Lord and Father, we thank You for this time around the communion table. Thank You that You make all things new. Thank You for the victory and power that is in Your name. Thank You that You hold the keys over death; that by Your might, Jesus was raised from the grave, paving the way for us to have new life with You.

As we see the days lengthen and the promise of new life in Your created world, we thank You most of all that You have given us new life in the Lord Jesus; that though He died, He is alive and reigning with You in heaven.

Lord, we confess our need for You again. We ask that You might renew our hearts, minds and lives for the days ahead. By Your Spirit fill us again with the expectation of Jesus' return and the knowledge of Your love in salvation; and may our lives of service overflow to Your praise and glory. Amen.

Grace to redeem
a wretch

Do you enjoy words? I love them. 'Grace' 'redeem' and 'wretch' are some of my favourites. We communicate so much through words.

From Bible times to the present day, the idea of redemption has had a great influence on Jewish theology. The memory of the exodus from Egypt has been absorbed into Jewish thought, and life is shaped by this event. The Passover Haggadah states, 'In every single generation it is a man's duty to regard himself as if he came out of Egypt.'

Modern-day Jews believe they are redeemed through prayer, worship, study and acts of loving-kindness. As Shlomo Yitzchaki (Rashi), an influential medieval commentator on the Talmud, stated, 'What really matters is that one's heart is directed to God, a framing that expresses God's appreciation for the Jewish people's obedience.' This is in stark contrast to the Christian understanding of Scripture. We depend on grace alone through faith for our redemption.

Songwriters down the years have used their skill with words to help us lift our hearts, minds and voices to God. One of the most prolific hymnwriters was the ex-slave ship captain John Newton. As he contemplated God's grace in his life and his own past behaviour, he considered himself wretched and famously wrote the line: 'Amazing grace! how sweet the sound, that saved a wretch like me.'

More recently, Stuart Townend borrowed the word 'wretch' for one of his songs:

How deep the Father's love for us,

How vast beyond all measure,

That He should give His only Son

To make a wretch His treasure.

(Stuart Townend © 1995 Thankyou Music)

'Wretch' isn't an easy word to think about, but to fully appreciate words like 'ransomed' and 'redeemed' we need to have understood and come to terms with the description of ourselves as a 'wretch'. We must confess that it was because of our sins, past, present and future, that Christ hung on the cross. It was because our sin was so serious that, while it was being punished, Father and Son were separated and the sky was darkened over the earth.

So how can we who are only too aware of our sins, despite being followers of Jesus, be permitted to sit at the Lord's table? Can someone come to the table who has denied their Lord? Can those come who have ducked the issues of faith and run rather than stood up for what they believe?

According to Matthew's record of the night Jesus was betrayed, there were three incidents we can relate to as we consider our unworthiness to come into the presence of Jesus. In Matthew 26:21 Jesus warns them: 'Truly I tell you, one of you will betray me.' A few verses later in the chapter he says, 'This very night, before the cock crows, you will disown me three times' (v. 34). And then it is recorded in verse 56: 'all the disciples deserted him and fled'.

Yet it was on that same night, knowing that He would be betrayed, denied and abandoned, that He washed His disciples' feet. On this very night He gave them the teaching about bread and wine, giving to the church these sacraments: visible, tangible symbols of His body broken and His lifeblood poured out. This love feast that has strengthened and encouraged millions of Christians down the centuries was inaugurated in the knowledge that His disciples would let Him down in the hours ahead.

> Oh how the grace of God
> Amazes me!
> It loosed me from my bonds
> And set me free!
>
> . . .
>
> Amazed, I wonder why,
> He, the sinless one, should die
> For one so vile as I:
> My Saviour He!
> (Emmanuel Sibomana, c.1910–1975; tr. Rosemary
> Guillebaud © Church Missionary Society)

Since we last gathered at this table, which of us has not, in some way, grieved our Lord? Maybe not as Judas did, but have we, by speaking or remaining silent, denied or deserted Him? It is still His way to build the church with frail and fallible people like us. It is still His joy to nourish our souls at His table.

> Come to this sacred Table, not because you must, but because you may:
> Come to testify not that you are righteous, but that you

sincerely love our Lord Jesus Christ, and desire to be His true disciples:

Come, not because you are strong, but because you are weak;

Not because you have any claim on Heaven's rewards, but because in your frailty and sin you stand in constant need of Heaven's mercy and help:

Come, not to express an opinion, but to seek a Presence and pray for a Spirit.

And now that the Supper of the Lord is spread before you,

Lift up your minds and hearts above all selfish fears and cares;

Let this bread and this wine be to you the witnesses and signs of the grace of our Lord Jesus Christ, the love of God, and the communion of the Holy Spirit.

Before the Throne of the Heavenly Father and the Cross of the Redeemer make your humble confession of sin,

Consecrate your lives to the Christian obedience and service, and pray for strength to do and to bear the holy and blessed will of God.[1]

As we come to the table of the Lord, let us confess that we are unworthy. Let us praise Him that He has made us wretches His treasure! And let us respond with joy to Christ's invitation to dine with Him, rejoicing in the free gifts of salvation and eternal life that are ours through Him.

Prayer

> *Almighty God, unto whom all hearts be open, all desires known, and from whom no secrets are hid: cleanse the thoughts of our hearts by the inspiration of thy Holy Spirit, that we may perfectly love thee, and worthily magnify your holy Name; through Christ our Lord. Amen.*
>
> ('Collect for Purity', Book of Common Prayer)

Sitting next to Jesus

For where two or three gather in my name, there am I
with them. (Matt. 18:20)

At the table of the Lord, we speak of meeting with Him,
just as He met with his disciples in the breaking of bread
at that first Passover meal.

We know that Jesus is here with us by His Spirit as He
promised, but if we could see Jesus here with us physically,
wouldn't we want to sit close to Him? Wouldn't we want
to hear His least whisper, to gaze on His face, to see the
compassion in His eyes, to watch every movement of those
nail-pierced hands? How precious that would be.

In Mark 10 we read that James and John asked if they could
sit at the right and left hands of Jesus when He came into His
kingdom. But their motivation was not primarily love for Him,
but pride and a desire for their own glory.

Ironically, just before they made this request, Jesus had
reiterated the importance of humility, telling them, 'Many
who are first will be last, and the last first' (Mark 10:31).

The other disciples were indignant. But was that because
of the arrogance of the sons of Zebedee, or because they too
wanted pride of place at the table? 'You don't know what
you are asking,' Jesus said. 'Whoever wants to become great
among you must be your servant, and whoever wants to be
first must be slave of all. For even the Son of Man did not come
to be served, but to serve, and to give his life as a ransom for
many' (10:38, 43–45).

James and John did eventually learn the balance between

godly ambition and humility. James was the first of the disciples to be martyred by Herod Agrippa—the only apostle whose death is recorded in the New Testament. And John's humility is one of the great virtues that comes through in his writings. Throughout his Gospel, he never once mentions his own name, as doing so might focus attention on him. Instead, he refers to himself as 'the disciple whom Jesus loved', giving glory to Jesus.

Also, only John's Gospel records in detail Jesus' act of washing the disciples' feet. It is clear that at the Last Supper, Jesus' own humility on the night of His betrayal made a lasting impression on John.

If Jesus were to come into our congregation right now, where do you think He would choose to sit? Would He swagger to the most honoured place, or would He sit with the poorest, the least person in the eyes of the world? Sometimes our eyes and our values are corrupted by the world in which we live and its material standards.

If we want to sit with Jesus, should we not sit with the poor, the suffering and the downtrodden, because that's where He would choose to be?

> You laid aside Your majesty,
> Gave up everything for me,
> Suffered at the hands of those You had created.
> You took all my guilt and shame,
> When You died and rose again;
> Now today You reign,

In heaven and earth exalted.

. . .

You are the only one who died for me,

Gave Your life to set me free,

So I lift my voice to You in adoration.

(Noel Richards © 1985 Thankyou Music)

Jesus is the greatest example of humility. He, the Lord of all, humbled Himself and was born into squalor, became a refugee and lived in poverty. The Creator of the universe gave Himself in the service of His creatures and submitted Himself to their unjust cruelty. And finally He gave His life so that we might have life eternal!

Prayer

O Lord and heavenly Father, we your servants entirely desire your fatherly goodness mercifully to accept this our sacrifice of praise and thanksgiving, and to grant that, by the merits and death of your Son Jesus Christ, and through faith in his blood, we and all your Church may receive forgiveness of our sins and all other benefits of his passion.

And here we offer and present to you, O Lord, ourselves, our souls and bodies, to be a reasonable, holy, and living sacrifice, humbly beseeching you that all we who are partakers of this holy communion may be fulfilled with your grace and heavenly benediction.

And although we are unworthy, through our many sins, to offer you any sacrifice, yet we pray that you will accept this, the duty and service that we owe, not weighing our merits, but pardoning our offences, through Jesus Christ our Lord, by whom, and with whom, in the unity of the Holy Spirit, all honour and glory be yours, Father almighty, now and for ever. Amen.

(Book of Common Prayer)

Between times— counting the omer

For no matter how many promises God has made, they are 'Yes' in Christ. And so through him the 'Amen' is spoken by us to the glory of God. (2 Cor. 1:20)

D
o you find unresolved issues difficult? I do. While we're waiting for something to be completed there's always a measure of uncertainty about the outcome. We are people of the immediate, and it is often hard to wait patiently.

In the Jewish calendar the fifty days between Passover and Pentecost (Shavuot) are counted. This is the period when the children of Israel were in the wilderness between leaving Egypt and reaching Mount Sinai, where they were given the law and where God renewed with Moses the covenant he had made with Abraham.

The first grain to ripen at Passover was the barley, and every day until the wheat ripened fifty days later an 'omer', or half a gallon of barley, was cut and taken to the temple in a bowl and presented to God as an act of thanksgiving. After the fifty days, the firstfruits of the wheat harvest were offered. This was called 'counting the omer', and the instruction comes in Leviticus 23:16: 'Count fifty days up to the day after the seventh Sabbath, and then present an offering of new grain to the LORD.' Jewish people still symbolically 'count the omer', but this now just means a counting of the days.

For the children of Israel, the time in the wilderness was filled with uncertainty. They knew of the covenant God had made with Abraham around four hundred years earlier, but they were not yet in the land of promise. They showed their uncertainty by questioning, complaining and even turning to idols.

After Jesus' death and resurrection at Easter the disciples also were confused and uncertain. They had seen the miracle of His resurrection and had been promised the coming of the Holy Spirit, having been told to wait in Jerusalem until that time, but they had no idea how long they would have to wait. It must have been a long fifty days until Pentecost.

Twenty-first-century Christians live between the ascension and the second coming of Jesus, when the history of the world will be resolved. Christ's return has been clearly promised but, like the early disciples, we have no idea how long we will need to wait. At times we are so concerned with the immediate that we forget we are to watch and wait expectantly for His coming.

The verse in 2 Corinthians quoted at the start of this chapter reminds us that because all God's promises are 'Yes' in Christ Jesus, we can give our 'Amen' to them.

As we come to the communion table in thankful remembrance of Christ's sacrifice for my sin and yours, we can remember that, although history is unresolved, we can have security in our salvation—no uncertainty.

> There is a hope that burns within my heart,
>
> That gives me strength for every passing day;
>
> A glimpse of glory now revealed in meagre part,
>
> Yet drives all doubt away:
>
> I stand in Christ, with sins forgiven;

And Christ in me, the hope of heaven!
My highest calling and my deepest joy,
To make His will my home.
(Stuart Townend & Mark Edwards
© 2007 Thankyou Music)

We also wait in expectation of His coming again having the promise given by the angels to the first disciples at the ascension: 'This same Jesus, who has been taken from you into heaven, will come back in the same way you have seen him go into heaven' (Acts 1:11). The promise is repeated in Hebrews 9:28: 'Christ was sacrificed once to take away the sins of many; and he will appear a second time, not to bear sin, but to bring salvation to those who are waiting for him.'

Prayer

Lord Jesus, we thank You once again for this time around Your table, remembering Your atoning sacrifice for us so long ago.

We thank You also that as we have taken the bread and wine, You have nourished our souls in faith with Your body and blood.

We gladly proclaim our confidence that You will come again and fulfil Your promise to gather all the redeemed.

Lord, send us out into the world with joy in our hearts, the message of hope on our lips, and our eyes on Your coming kingdom. Amen.

Pentecost
Sunday

This is the covenant I will establish with the people of Israel after that time, declares the Lord. I will put my laws in their minds and write them on their hearts. I will be their God, and they will be my people. (Heb. 8:10)

In Israel, three harvest festivals are celebrated each year. These festivals are times when religious celebrations also take place. They are the early barley harvest in the spring at Passover, the wheat harvest fifty days later at Pentecost, and the fruit harvest in the autumn at the Feast of Tabernacles.

The term 'Pentecost' comes from the Greek (*pentēkostē*) meaning 'fiftieth'. This refers to the period between Passover, when the children of Israel celebrated their freedom from slavery in Egypt, and the giving of the law fifty days later: the rules within which they were to live.

Jewish people use the Hebrew word *shavuot*, meaning 'weeks', rather than 'Pentecost'. This festival is also known as the 'Feast of Weeks/Firstfruits', and being the celebration of the beginning of the early wheat harvest, Pentecost always falls sometime during the middle of May or sometimes in early June.

In temple times farmers would take the firstfruits of their wheat, grapes, figs, olives, pomegranates and date honey and lay them beside the altar in gratitude to God (Deut. 26:2–4). To celebrate Shavuot today, beautiful floral arrangements are hung in synagogues, and embroidered green curtains are hung over the ark where the Torah (Pentateuch) scroll is stored.

At this season observant Jews all around the world will stay up the entire night discussing and studying the Torah. They have breaks for coffee and cake during the night to help them stay awake and alert. Discussion revolves around the opening and closing verses of each book of the Bible, and the entire book of Ruth is read, as the events recorded there occurred at harvest time. On the following morning in Israel thousands of Jews make their way to the site of the temple at the Western Wall Plaza, where they stand and pray the silent prayer known in Hebrew as the 'Amidah' (literally 'the standing').

Whilst for the Jew the fifty days represent the time between leaving slavery in Egypt and receiving the law through Moses at Sinai, for Christians the days represent the time between the event at Easter that set them free from the slavery of sin, and Pentecost fifty days later, when they were given the law of love in their hearts through the power of the Holy Spirit.

Sadly, in their studies of the details of the law, the Jewish people failed to see the One who had given it. They couldn't see that the law showed them their inability to keep it and pointed to the One who would one day come to fulfil it. They were looking for a king, and when Jesus came as a servant they didn't recognize Him for who He was; and they missed the significance of His death and resurrection and His demonstration of the power of God over sin and death.

Pentecost is sometimes called the birthday of the church. However, the messianic scholar at All Nations Christian College, Martin Goldsmith, comments,

I have heard this unbiblical assertion repeated over and over again like a mantra which is said so often that it is finally accepted as 'obviously true'. Actually the New Testament carefully chose the Greek word *ekklesia* for 'church' because it is the word used in the LXX (the Greek translation of the Old Testament which is commonly used in the New Testament) for *Qahal*, the congregation of Israel. The church is the continuation of the people of Israel, but now with Gentiles added into Israel's olive tree. We are of course reminded of Romans 11's picture of Gentile branches being added to the tree of Israel. So, when is the birthday of the church? When was Israel's birthday? The call of Abraham? Or even creation?[1]

Acts 2 records that historic occasion when the Holy Spirit was poured out on the disciples. As a result of them speaking of the mighty works of God in as many languages as there were people groups, three thousand people believed in Jesus and were baptized and added to the church.

For us at the feast of Pentecost, the Holy Spirit coming upon the church is seen as the fulfilment of the shadow of the law given in the book of Leviticus. And as the Jews celebrate the harvest of firstfruits, so we celebrate the empowering of the church to bring in the harvest of the gospel. Since that day recorded in Acts 2 many millions of people all around the world have found freedom from sin through Jesus.

The coming of the Holy Spirit replaced the rule of law with

the rule of grace. The amazing grace of God is seen in His power to forgive our sins.

Let us come to the table of the Lord remembering with thankfulness that we are no longer slaves to sin, unable to make ourselves right with God or to resist the temptations of the evil one. Now, in Christ, we have the freedom to choose good over evil and right over wrong!

Let us feed on Him in our hearts.

Prayer

We praise You, heavenly Father, because You are holy. We rejoice in the plan of salvation set out since the beginning of time and foreshadowed throughout Scripture—Your plan in which You would send Your beloved Son into the world to redeem fallen mankind.

Thank You, Lord Jesus, that You were willing to take the curse for us. By faith we have met once again with You, our risen and living Lord.

We thank You, Holy Spirit, for guiding us into salvation, for renewing our dead spirits and for opening our eyes to the truth. Thank You for dwelling in our hearts and working in our lives.

This Pentecost, pour out your Spirit on us afresh so we might live lives of joyful service for You. Amen.

Christmas/Migdal Eder: 'The tower of the flock'

Both shepherds and lambs feature throughout Scripture, and we are familiar with references to Jesus being the Lamb of God and also the Good Shepherd. So it is not insignificant that the first people to visit Jesus at His birth were shepherds and that Jesus was born near 'the tower of the flock', or Migdal Eder.

We first read of the place called Migdal Eder in Genesis, when Jacob's wife, Rachel, died giving birth to Benjamin and was buried on the way to Bethlehem: 'So Rachel died and was buried on the way to Ephrath (that is, Bethlehem). Over her tomb Jacob set up a pillar, and to this day that pillar marks Rachel's tomb. Israel moved on again and pitched his tent beyond Migdal Eder' (Gen. 35:19–21).

Much later, Micah prophesied about the future birth of Israel's Messiah. He predicted the reappearance of God's kingdom at Migdal Eder, the tower of the flock:

> As for you, watchtower of the flock,
>   stronghold of Daughter Zion,
> the former dominion will be restored to you;
>   kingship will come to Daughter Jerusalem. (Micah 4:8)

> But you, Bethlehem Ephrathah,
>   though you are small among the clans of Judah,
> out of you will come for me
>   one who will be ruler over Israel,
> whose origins are from of old,
>   from ancient times . . .

. . .

until the time when she who is in labour bears a son . . .

. . .

He will stand and shepherd his flock

. . .

And they will live securely, for then his greatness
will reach to the ends of the earth.

And he will be our peace. (Micah 5:2–5)

It is not just Christians who believe that these verses refer to the coming of the Messiah. Based on this prophecy, prominent Jewish writers concluded in the Midrash (sacred writings on the Hebrew Scriptures) that from all of the places in Israel, it would be Migdal Eder where the arrival of the Messiah would be declared first. They believed the Messiah would be born in Bethlehem and would be revealed from the 'tower of the flock'.

Passover lambs were kept by specially trained and purified shepherds on the outskirts of Bethlehem. The lambs were born in this 'tower of the flock' under the watchful eye of the shepherds who would then inspect them and either certify them for use as sacrifices in the temple or designate them to be released for common use.

So perhaps it is no surprise that Jesus was born in the shadow of Migdal Eder! Nor that it was the shepherds in the fields of Bethlehem, whose task was to care for the sheep who would supply the sacrificial system of the temple, who were the first to be told of the birth of the Messiah. These were the shepherds who were now confronted with the perfect Lamb their ministry had been pointing to for centuries. The Saviour had come!

In that prophecy in Micah we are told that the Promised One would shepherd His flock, that His greatness would reach the ends of the earth, and that He would bring peace. And when the angels brought the message of the Saviour's birth to the shepherds, they must have been reminded of the promise as they heard their song: 'Glory to God in the highest heaven, and on earth peace to those on whom his favour rests' (Luke 2:14). The 'Prince of Peace' prophesied by Isaiah (Isa. 9:6) had come!

How was that peace with God achieved? Through the One who described Himself as the Good Shepherd becoming the sacrificial Lamb of God. We come to the table of the Lord knowing that through this sacrifice we have peace with God. Glory to God in the highest!

Prayer

Loving Father, help us remember the birth of Jesus, that we may share in the song of the angels, the gladness of the shepherds, and worship of the wise men.

Close the door of hate and open the door of love all over the world. Let kindness come with every gift and good desires with every greeting. Deliver us from evil by the blessing which Christ brings, and teach us to be merry with clear hearts.

May the Christmas morning make us happy to be thy

children, and the Christmas evening bring us to our beds with grateful thoughts, forgiving and forgiven, for Jesus' sake. Amen.

('A Christmas Prayer' attributed to Robert Louis Stevenson)

Why communion?

How good and pleasant it is
  when God's people live together in unity!
It is like precious oil poured on the head,
  running down on the beard,
running down on Aaron's beard,
  down on the collar of his robe.
It is as if the dew of Hermon
  were falling on Mount Zion.
For there the Lord bestows his blessing,
  even life for evermore. (Ps. 133:1–3)

Why do we celebrate communion? Some churches meet together every two weeks, others weekly, some twice a year after preparation services. Christian groups over the centuries have disagreed—sometimes violently—over the meanings and implications of this simple meal. It seems a lot hangs on a morsel of bread and a sip of grape juice.

Jesus thought it was important. At His last teaching of the disciples at the Passover meal He told them that all disciples should do it to remember Him. The reports in the Acts of the Apostles suggest that the early church met together regularly to break bread, and Paul thought it important enough to devote a section of 1 Corinthians to it.

There is much in the Bible to understand and much in the Christian life to consider and learn about. We find comfort in the promises of God to His people, strength to face bad times, and joy in the many blessings He gives. We also learn of the cost of being a follower of Jesus, but are promised a great reward in heaven when we face persecution. As we rejoice together over these truths we find unity. But most important of all is that we find unity as we come around the Lord's table.

Of course, we know that Christians have different opinions about many things: the end times, methods of baptism, how the Holy Spirit works in our lives, church government, and many other things. These things could unsettle us if we didn't have a fixed reference point, a fact that unites all believers.

> Now, brothers and sisters, I want to remind you of the gospel I preached to you, which you received and on which you have taken your stand. By this gospel you are saved, if you hold firmly to the word I preached to you. Otherwise, you have believed in vain.

> For what I received I passed on to you as of first importance: that Christ died for our sins according to the Scriptures, that he was buried, that he was raised on the third day according to the Scriptures. (1 Cor. 15:1–4)

In this passage Paul bring us back to that solid reference point, the pivotal point in human history: Jesus died for our sins on the cross. It is by this good news that we are saved, and all who hold firmly to this word are one in Him.

'We are invited to come together around this table as those who belong to the household of Christ, brothers and sisters who in our baptized lives live out the death and resurrection of Jesus. The family of the reborn and the reconciled, who inhabit a universe of grace' (Baptist Union).[1]

We believe in the Lord Jesus Christ, who entered time; God born in human flesh, who lived a sinless life, died in our place, and took the just punishment for our sins on the cross. And having conquered death, He rose in power on the third day.

That is why we come frequently to the communion table. This table causes us to return to the foundations of our faith, to remember the centrality of the cross. This is where we come to that pivotal moment of human history—but one that is so personal to each and every Christian.

> [We] are the family of God,
>
> [We] are the promise divine,
>
> [We] are God's chosen desire,
>
> [We] are the glorious new wine.

> Made for the glory of God,
>
> Purchased by His precious Son;
>
> Born with the right to be clean,
>
> For Jesus the victory has won!

Prayer

As we have shared bread and wine in your presence, Lord Jesus, you have renewed our faith and hope.

As we go out into a new week, we pray that your power will protect us, your love and mercy comfort us, and your Holy Spirit guide our steps.

Make us fervent in praise, diligent in duty, slow to anger and quick to forgive. And may our lives leave some fragrance of you, Lord Jesus, wherever we go.

'Cleanse me with hyssop'

Cleanse me with hyssop, and I will be clean;

wash me, and I shall be whiter than snow. (Ps. 51:7)

As we come to the communion table we remind ourselves once again of our own sin and frailty, of the perfection and purity of Jesus, and of our salvation through Him. We have been made clean through His shed blood and are free from the guilt and punishment of our sin. But we also need to come again and again to say with King David, 'Cleanse me.'

Hyssop is a herb in the mint family and has cleansing, medicinal and flavouring properties. The Bible mentions hyssop several times, mostly in the Old Testament, as something used in the ceremonial cleansing of people and houses.

Leviticus 14 sets out the regulations for dealing with any defiling skin disease or sore, any moulds in fabric or in a house, and a swelling, rash or shiny spot. If a person had been recently healed from a skin disease, God told the priests to use hyssop, together with cedar wood, scarlet yarn and the blood of a clean bird, and sprinkle it over the person. This act would ceremonially cleanse the formerly diseased person and allow him or her to re-enter the camp. The same method was used to purify a house that had previously contained mould.

Hyssop is also used symbolically in the Bible. The Israelites were instructed to use a bunch of hyssop as a 'paintbrush' to mark their doorposts with the lamb's blood so that the angel of death would pass over them (Exod. 12:22). God was marking

His people as 'pure' and not targets of the judgement He was about to visit on the Egyptians.

When we celebrate Passover these days we eat a piece of parsley or similar green vegetable, called *karpas* in Hebrew, to represent the hyssop that was used to daub the blood of the paschal lamb on the doorposts and lintel of the house. Traditionally it is dipped in salt water to represent the tears the Israelite slaves shed while in Egypt.

Hyssop also appears at Jesus' crucifixion, when the Roman soldiers offered Jesus a drink of wine vinegar on a sponge at the end of a stalk of hyssop (John 19:28–30). While the hyssop stalk may have been used for purely practical reasons because it was long enough to reach Jesus' mouth as He hung on the cross, maybe it's not insignificant that this particular plant was chosen. It is possible that God meant this as a picture of purification, as Jesus bought our forgiveness with His sacrifice.

In the days before Jesus died He gave many words of encouragement to His followers. What a comfort these words must have been to them at that time and in the days after He had returned to heaven: 'You are already clean because of the word I have spoken to you' (John 15:3). Later in his epistle the apostle wrote: 'If we walk in the light, as he is in the light, we have fellowship with one another, and the blood of Jesus, his Son, purifies us from all sin' (1 John 1:7).

Amazingly, these words apply to us too if we are trusting in Jesus for forgiveness.

Rock of Ages, cleft for me,

Let me hide myself in Thee;
Let the water and the blood,
From Thy riven side which flowed,
Be of sin the double cure:
Cleanse me from its guilt and power.

Nothing in my hand I bring;
Simply to Thy cross I cling.
Naked, come to Thee for dress;
Helpless, look to Thee for grace;
Foul, I to the fountain fly;
Wash me, Saviour, or I die.
(Augustus Toplady, 1776)

Just as in the Old Testament blood and hyssop purified a defiled person, so Jesus' shed blood purifies us from the defilement of our sin. Let us apply the blood to the doorposts of our hearts by putting our trust in the work of Jesus, our Passover Lamb.

Prayer

Eternal God and Father,
by whose power we are created and by whose love we are redeemed:
guide and strengthen us by your Spirit,
that we may give ourselves to your service,
and live this day in love to one another and to you;
through Jesus Christ your Son our Lord. Amen.
(An Australian Prayer Book)[1]

Lord Jesus Christ, thank You that You became cursed for us, for by Your stripes we are healed and by Your death we are made alive.

God and Father, thank You for this time of remembrance and spiritual nourishment as we are fed by faith on the bread and the wine. Amen.

Look
and live!

See what great love the Father has lavished on us, that
we should be called children of God! And that is what
we are! . . . Dear friends, now we are children of God,
and what we will be has not yet been made known. But
we know that when Christ appears, we shall be like
him, for we shall see him as he is. (1 John 3:1–2)

We live in a celebrity culture where the important thing is
to be in the public gaze and get attention from others.
Sadly, many look at so-called 'celebrities' to model their own
behaviour and values. The things we look at and the things
that take our attention show what we are interested in. What
we gaze at reveals what we revere.

When Jesus spoke to Nicodemus he reminded him of the
story of Abraham and the bronze serpent. As the children of
Israel were travelling through the wilderness,

> they grew impatient on the way; they spoke against
> God and against Moses, and said, 'Why have you
> brought us up out of Egypt to die in the wilderness?
> There is no bread! There is no water! And we detest
> this miserable food!'

> Then the LORD sent venomous snakes among them;
> they bit the people and many Israelites died. The
> people came to Moses and said, 'We sinned when we
> spoke against the LORD and against you. Pray that the
> LORD will take the snakes away from us.' So Moses
> prayed for the people.

> The LORD said to Moses, 'Make a snake and put it up
> on a pole; anyone who is bitten can look at it and live.'
> So Moses made a bronze snake and put it up on a pole.
> Then when anyone was bitten by a snake and looked
> at the bronze snake, they lived. (Num. 21:4–9)

The children of Israel were being bitten by serpents because of their sin, but in His mercy God instructed Moses to make a bronze serpent and set it on a pole so that anyone who had been bitten who looked at the bronze snake was healed.

Jesus explained to Nicodemus that if he sincerely desired eternal life, he needed to look to the Son of Man who would be lifted up, and believe in Him (John 3:14).

We are urged by the writer to the Hebrews to lay aside every sin and look to Jesus, the author and finisher of our faith. I like the NIV translation of this verse: 'fixing our eyes on Jesus, the pioneer and perfecter of faith' (Heb. 12:2). It is not just glancing at Jesus occasionally or looking at Him on a Sunday; fixing our eyes on Him suggests a more deliberate gaze, in the same way as the children of Israel gazed on the bronze snake to be healed.

And just as the children of Israel could look and live, so must we if we are to receive eternal life. We cannot strive to save ourselves. We cannot look at others to find life, nor can we look to our own efforts. Our faith can't be manufactured; it comes only as our souls gaze on Christ. As we gaze on Him, we see Him for who He is, and we are transformed.

In 1 John 3 we are invited to look and see the great love

the Father has lavished on us, that we can be called children of God. What an amazing privilege to be called children of God because of what Jesus accomplished for us at Calvary! How can it be possible that undeserving sinners, worthy only of judgement and condemnation, can become children of God? It is only because of the Father's great love that sent His Son to take our place—that steadfast love poured out for us.

> To the cross, to the cross,
> Spirit lead me to the cross.
> Bowed in awe at His feet,
> Richest gain I count as loss.
> Nothing compares with this,
> To share His righteousness,
> And be called a child of God.
> To the cross, to the cross
> Spirit lead me to the cross.
> (Geoff Baker © 1998 Daybreak Music Ltd)

As we come to the Lord's table, let us look and consider that unending, unconditional, sacrificial, saving, sanctifying love! We can trust in the steadfast nature of this love and be secure because of the nature of God, which cannot change.

The more we look on Jesus, the more we will be transformed into His likeness. The transformation is partial now. We remain in bodies that ache, fail and decay. We are still sinful, our thoughts, words and deeds being corrupted with our old nature. But we know that when Christ appears we will shall see Him as He is—see with perfect clarity, our gaze fixed on the author and finisher of our faith. The One who died in our place, who took our punishment and has gone ahead to prepare a place for us, will finish the job of making us like Him. We will be like Jesus!

Prayer

> *Father of all,*
> *we give you thanks and praise,*
> *that when we were still far off*
> *you met us in your Son and brought us home.*
> *Dying and living, he declared your love,*
> *gave us grace, and opened the gate of glory.*
> *May we who share Christ's body live his risen life;*
> *we who drink his cup bring life to others;*
> *we whom the Spirit lights give light to the world.*
> *Keep us firm in the hope you have set before us,*
> *so we and all your children shall be free,*
> *and the whole earth live to praise your name;*
> *through Christ our Lord.*
> *Amen.*
>
> ('Prayer after Communion')[1]

Jesus, cursed Redeemer

Anyone who is hung on a pole [or 'tree'] is under God's curse. (Deut. 21:23)

The famous Chinese general Sun Tzu, in his book *The Art of War*, wrote extensively about deception. He said that when you are weak you should appear strong, and when you are strong you should appear weak.

Joshua used this method of deception when fighting against Ai, as recorded in Joshua 8. He sent a section of Israel's army to lie in wait behind the city while he and the rest of the fighting men approached it. When the enemy came out against them, Joshua pretended to be beaten and he and the men with him fled into the wilderness. The king of Ai and his army were drawn away from the city so that the men lying in wait were able to ambush the city and win the battle.

The Jews knew that under the law of Moses, anyone hanged on a tree was under God's curse. They were familiar with the words in Deuteronomy 21:22–23: 'If someone guilty of a capital offence is put to death and their body is exposed on a pole . . . be sure to bury it that same day, because anyone who is hung on a pole [or 'tree'] is under God's curse.' The law made it illegal to leave such a body hanging overnight. This law applied to Jesus, who was executed on a tree although He had done no wrong. Jesus' dead body was removed from the cross on the same day of His death and was buried.

So when the enemies of Jesus managed to get the Romans to crucify Jesus, they were triumphant. He appeared so weak, and made no attempt to prove His innocence. It was a victory for the establishment. The kingdom of darkness thought it had won. Jesus was not only dead, but hung on a tree—cursed by God.

It seemed to the disciples that all was lost. Jesus had been defeated, the one who was to redeem Israel totally humiliated. How could a 'cursed one' be 'God's chosen one'? For the disciples, there was confusion and despair—until the resurrection.

Years later, the Apostle Paul explained it like this: 'Christ redeemed us from the curse of the law by becoming a curse for us, for it is written: "Cursed is everyone who is hung on a pole"' (Gal. 3:13). Jesus hung on the cross as a substitute for our sins and took the curse upon Himself to redeem us from sin. After the resurrection, the disciples realized that in the battle between good and evil the enemy had been deceived. Jesus had ambushed and defeated death.

Our Lord Jesus became the 'cursed one' for us. Yes, He really did die. Just the physical suffering of that cruellest of executions would have been bad enough, but He also bore a much greater pain—the punishment of God for your sins and mine.

He took the punishment of all our sin and wrongdoing and in so doing won the war with sin and death.

The NIV has entitled Isaiah 35 'Joy of the redeemed' as the passage describes the joy of the ransomed of Israel. It is our song of redemption too if we have put our trust in Him and the sacrifice of His own life as a ransom for ours. We are the redeemed! We can join in the song:

And a highway will be there;

  it will be called the Way of Holiness;

  it will be for those who walk on that Way.

. . .

Only the redeemed will walk there,

  and those the LORD has rescued will return.

They will enter Zion with singing;

  everlasting joy will crown their heads.

Gladness and joy will overtake them,

  and sorrow and sighing will flee away. (Isa. 35:8–10)

He rose again, victorious as our Redeemer! This was the plan made before all time—the reason why He came. This is our Lord and Saviour whom we remember.

Prayer

Thank You, Lord Jesus, for this simple meal, enjoyed by Your followers since the earliest times of the church.

We thank and praise You for Your death in our place; that You were willing to take the curse that should have been ours so that we might be redeemed; for that resurrection power that showed Your mastery over death and hell; and for Your grace that enables us to come to You in faith.

Guide and strengthen us by Your Spirit so that, understanding the wonder of the cross, we may give ourselves to Your service, to live this day and every day in love for one another and for You. Amen.

Feast of
Tabernacles

Around October, Jewish people celebrate Sukkot, commonly translated from the Hebrew as 'Feast of Tabernacles' or 'Feast of Booths'. It comes at the time of the autumn fruit harvest and is also sometimes referred to as the 'Festival of Ingathering' as it marks the end of the harvest time and thus of the agricultural year in the land of Israel. The holiday lasts seven days in Israel and eight in the diaspora.

During the existence of the Jerusalem temple, it was one of the Three Pilgrimage Festivals when the Israelites were commanded to perform a pilgrimage to Jerusalem. Water libation was performed at the temple, after the high priest had led a procession from the Pool of Siloam back to the temple. Water was poured over the altar in a special ceremony giving thanks for the spring rains that had enabled the harvest and praying for the autumn rains to come. It was celebrated with great joy, music, dancing and singing.

The Jewish people built temporary shelters and lived in them for seven days to remember that they once dwelled in temporary shelters in the wilderness, totally dependent on the Lord. As stated in Leviticus 23, the shelters were intended as a reminder of the type of fragile dwelling in which the Israelites lived during their forty years of travel in the desert after the exodus from slavery. It was to be at once a thanksgiving for the harvest and a commemoration of the time when they dwelt in tents in the wilderness.

Orthodox Jewish families today build these makeshift huts (*sukkot*) on their patios and balconies, and decorate them with colourful fruit, leaves, ribbons and pictures. I remember our family building such a hut. It had gaps in the roof so that we could see the stars. We ate our meals inside the *sukkah*, and my brother even slept there for the eight nights. One year we had snow in October, but he still slept outside!

In John's Gospel we read of the time when Jesus taught in the temple courts during the Feast of Tabernacles. Imagine the scene. There would have been crowds of people, and water libations taking place all around, when Jesus stood up to make this astonishing declaration: 'Let anyone who is thirsty come to me and drink. Whoever believes in me, as Scripture has said, rivers of living water will flow from within them' (John 7:37–38).

As water is vital to the land, so is the Holy Spirit vital to the Christian. Water is a picture of blessing and life. As Jesus told the woman at the well: 'Whoever drinks the water I give them will never thirst. Indeed, the water I give them will become in them a spring of water welling up to eternal life' (John 4:14).

We come to this table aware of the redemption that Jesus won for us at Calvary. In the same way that Jesus confronted the Samaritan woman about her sin, His death reminds us of ours. As He comforted her with the truth of the gospel, we too are comforted. Even though He knows our sins, He has sought us and called us to be His children.

The Feast of Tabernacles is unique, in that the Gentile nations were invited to come up to Jerusalem along with the Jewish people to worship the Lord at this 'appointed time'.

The Lord told Moses to gather all men, women and children, along with the foreigners in their land, so that they might learn to fear the Lord (Deut. 31:12).

Let us gather round the table today remembering with gratitude all that Jesus did for us. Let us eat the bread and drink the cup feeding on Him in our hearts.

'The Spirit and the bride say, "Come!" And let the one who hears say, "Come!" Let the one who is thirsty come; and let the one who wishes take the free gift of the water of life' (Rev. 22:17).

Let us respond to this call and come again to the source of the water of life.

Prayer

Almighty and eternal God, as we approach the sacrament of the communion table to remember the Lord Jesus Christ, we come thirsty to the water of life and unclean to the fountain of mercy. Forgive us now, even the sins of this day and cleanse us as we repent of them.

May our hearts ever hunger after and feed upon You, whom the angels desire to look upon. May our inmost souls be filled with the sweetness of Your savour; may we ever thirst for You, the fountain of life, the fountain of wisdom and knowledge, the fountain of eternal light, the torrent of pleasure, the fullness of the house of God.

Be You alone our hope, our entire confidence, our riches, our delight, our rest, our possession, our refuge, our wisdom and our treasure. May our minds and hearts be ever fixed and firm and rooted immovably in You. Amen.[1]

Until He
come

> For whenever you eat this bread and drink this cup,
> you proclaim the Lord's death until he comes.
> (1 Cor. 11:26)

I have just celebrated Christmas with my family and enjoyed sitting together with everyone at the dining table eating our traditional Christmas fare. It was a very happy time.

At this time of year, however, Jewish people are celebrating Hanukkah, the festival of lights or 'Feast of Dedication', commemorating the rededication of the second temple in Jerusalem at the time of the Maccabean Revolt against the Seleucid Empire. It is a time of joy and fun, of giving and receiving gifts.

It was at the Feast of Dedication that, following Jesus' claim that He and the Father were one, the people reacted by trying to stone Him. Throughout the festival Jesus was effectively saying, 'You are having a festival of dedication, so will you dedicate yourselves to Me?'

Amid all the celebration, we know that even the most wonderful feast we may experience in this life is but a pale reflection of that much greater feast we will one day enjoy— the marriage feast of the Lamb.

The simple meal we are about to share is the hors d'oeuvre to that great feast. We who belong to Jesus are invited both to this table and to that feast to come. We will sit with Him there at His side!

But the feast in the future is possible only because of the sacrifice that was made in the past.

We come to the communion table to remind ourselves of what has been achieved for us by Christ's death on the cross. Not only were all our sins, past, present and future, dealt with, but also our citizenship was transferred. Once we were children of darkness; now we are children of the light. Our home is heaven, not earth; that is where our treasure is.

The communion service looks backwards and forwards: backwards to that pivotal act of eternity when Christ made sacrifice for our sins once for all, the just for the unjust; and forwards to that feast we have been thinking about, when we will rejoice in the presence of our Saviour for eternity.

As we take the bread and the wine, let us rededicate ourselves to Jesus. Here we are making a proclamation to the world: we are proud to be associated with Jesus. We come to proclaim the cross. We want to tell people that He is the only way; that His death bought our freedom. We are not offering a sacrifice again! We are visually proclaiming through broken bread and wine poured that what was done once for all is supremely important to us. What we do here is a proclamation—a temporary, visible rite to tell of that wonderful truth 'until he comes'.

> Here would I feed upon the bread of God,
> Here drink with Thee the royal wine of heaven;
> Here would I lay aside each earthly load,
> Here taste afresh the calm of sins forgiven.
>
> This is the hour of banquet and of song,
> This is the heavenly table spread for me;

Here let me feast, and, feasting, still prolong
The brief, bright hour of fellowship with Thee.

Too soon we rise, the symbols disappear;
The feast, though not the love, is past and gone;
The bread and wine remove, but Thou art here,
Nearer than ever still my Shield and Sun.

Feast after feast thus comes and passes by,
Yet, passing, points to the glad feast above,
Giving sweet foretastes of the festal joy,
The Lamb's great bridal feast of bliss and love.
(Horatius Bonar, 'Here, O My Lord,
I See Thee Face to Face', 1855)

Before us, in the bread, we have the word of God, the bread of life, made visible, tangible. We can know His presence at this table. The disciples on the Emmaus road didn't recognize Jesus, though He was right there. And as we gather in His name today we pray for our spiritual eyes to be opened so that we will recognize Him with us as never before. Then our hearts will thrill like a bride's as we look forward to that day when Christ will come for us and we will be at his side for ever.

John shares with us a glimpse of the day when the church will be presented to Christ as His bride:

> Then I heard what sounded like a great multitude, like the roar of rushing waters and like loud peals of thunder, shouting:

'Hallelujah!

For our Lord God Almighty reigns.

Let us rejoice and be glad

and give him glory!

For the wedding of the Lamb has come,

and his bride has made herself ready.

Fine linen, bright and clean,

was given her to wear.' . . .

'Blessed are those who are invited to the wedding supper of the Lamb!' (Rev. 19:6–9)

So we look forward to that point in time still to come: the time when Christ will come again and everything will be changed. On that day there will be no more communion services. When Jesus returns there will no longer be a need to proclaim Him, for we will be in His presence and will see Him in His glory. Those of us who are alive when He returns will not die but simply be transformed, and those who are dead will be raised and given new bodies. Every eye will see Him and every knee will bow. We will come to Him in the city of our God, the heaven which is our home.

All the church will be gathered around His table to praise Him for eternity.

As we come to take the bread and wine we look back, not to Egypt, the Passover meal that was the Last Supper, but to Calvary, where the Lord Jesus Christ brought us into that new covenant with Him. We look forward to sharing the marriage feast of the Lamb because death has been defeated by the Lamb of God.

At the conclusion of the Passover celebration these words are said: 'This year in exile, next year in Jerusalem. This year as slaves, next year as freemen.' For us at the end of this communion service we can say: 'This year in our temporary home, some day in the New Jerusalem! This year bound in earthen vessels, some day free to rise with Him!'

Prayer

Lord Jesus, thank You that this is a passing feast, temporary, until you come.

Thank You that each communion brings us one step closer to your return.

Thank You that You are coming.

Thank You for the promise of heaven we have in You.

We pray that the light of the glory to come will outshine the tawdry glitter of this world's attractions.

May God, Father, Son and Holy Spirit, guard our hearts and minds to keep all of our words and actions just and true, this week and for ever. Amen.

Conclusion

As we now, by eating the bread and drinking the drink in memory of the suffering and shed blood of our Lord Jesus Christ for the remission of our sins [we] have had fellowship with one another, and have all become one loaf and one body, and our head is Christ, we should properly become conformed to our Head and as his members follow after him, love one another, do good, give counsel, and be helpful to one another, each offering up his flesh and blood for the other . . .

Whereupon I pray and exhort you once more, most dearly beloved in Christ, that henceforth as table companions of Christ Jesus, you henceforth lead a Christian walk before God and before men. Be mindful of your baptismal commitment and of your pledge of love which you made to God and the church publicly . . . See to it that you bear fruit worthy of the baptism and the Supper of Christ, that you may in the power of God satisfy your pledge, promise, sacrament, and sworn commitment. God sees it and knows your hearts. May our Lord Jesus Christ, ever and eternally praised, grant us the same. Amen.
(Sixteenth-century Anabaptist communion service)[1]

Endnotes

Invitation

1 'Holy Communion Liturgy B', in *A Wee Worship Book* (Glasgow: Wild Goose Publications, 2015).

Chapter 1 Perfect sacrifice

1 United Methodist Church, *The United Methodist Book of Worship* (Nashville: Abingdon Press, 2016).

Chapter 2 Preparation

1 'Rosh Hashanah', BBC, last updated 23 September 2011, https://www.bbc.co.uk/religion/religions/judaism/holydays/roshhashanah.shtml/.

2 The Church of England, 'Holy Communion Order One', *Common Worship,* https://www.churchofengland.org/prayer-and-worship/worship-texts-and-resources/common-worship/churchs-year/holy-week-and-easter/holy-communion-order-one.

Chapter 3 Rosh Hashanah: Sound the trumpet

1 'Rosh Hashanah', BBC.

2 Ibid.

Chapter 4 Of first importance

1 John Calvin, *Institutes of the Christian Religion,* 17.42, https://www.ccel.org/ccel/calvin/institutes.vi.xviii.html.

Chapter 9 Our identity in Christ

1 'Holy Communion Order One', *Common Worship*.

Chapter 10 Feast of Unleavened Bread

1 The Church of England, 'Penitence', *Common Worship*, https://www.churchofengland.org/prayer-and-worship/worship-texts-and-resources/common-worship/common-material/new-patterns-worshp/resource-section-themes/b-penitence.

Chapter 11 Thoughts on the bread

1 'Holy Communion Order One', *Common Worship*.

Chapter 12 Passover cups

1 Book of Common Worship, Second Eucharistic Prayer.

2 Church of England, 'Easter', *Common Worship*, https://www.churchofengland.org/prayer-and-worship/worship-texts-and-resources/common-worship/churchs-year/times-and-seasons/easter.

Chapter 15 The new covenant between God and His people

1 'Eucharistic Prayer', Book of Common Worship.

Chapter 17 Easter firstfruits

1 'The Easter Anthems', *Common Worship*, from Rom. 6:9–11 and 1 Cor:15:20–22; https://www.churchofengland.org/prayer-and-worship/worship-texts-and-resources/common-worship/daily-prayer/canticles-daily-prayer/76-easter-anthems.

Chapter 18 Easter eggs

1 Anthony McRoy, 'How the Fast of Lent Gave Us Easter Eggs', *Christianity Today,* https://www.christianitytoday.com/history/2010/february/how-fast-of-lent-gave-us-easter-eggs.html.

2 Ibid.

3 'Easter Egg', Wikipedia, https://en.wikipedia.org/wiki/Easter_egg.

4 Ibid.

Chapter 19 In an unworthy manner?

1 Copyright © The Iona Community, from Iona Abbey Worship Book (2001 edition), published by Wild Goose Publications (www.ionabooks.com). Used with permission.

Chapter 24 Grace to redeem a wretch

1 John Hunter, *Devotional Services for Public Worship* (London: J. M. Dent, 1903).

Chapter 27 Pentecost Sunday

1 Martin Goldsmith, personal correspondence.

Chapter 29 Why communion?

1 Baptist Union of Great Britain, *Gathering for Worship: Patters and Prayers for the Community of Disciples* (Norwich: Canterbury Press, 2005).

Chapter 30 'Cleanse me with hyssop'

1 Quoted at 'Concluding Prayers and Blessings', Better Gatherings, http://www.bettergatherings.com/index.php?option=com_content&view=article&id=111&Itemid=99, copyright © 2020 Better Gatherings.

Chapter 31 Look and live!

1 'Holy Communion Order One', *Common Worship*.

Chapter 33 Feast of Tabernacles

1 Adapted from 'Prayer after Holy Communion: St Bonaventure', Liturgies.net, http://www.liturgies.net/Prayers/communion.htm.

Conclusion

1 Wayne Pipkin and John Yoder, *Balthasar Hubmaier* (Scottdale, PA: Herald Press, 1989), pp. 393–408, quoted in 'Balthasar Hubmaier: "A Form for Christ's Supper"', Anabaptist Mennonite Network, https://amnetwork.uk/resource/balthasar-hubmaier-a-form-for-christs-supper/.